healing death

healing death

Finding wholeness when a cure is no longer possible

Dennis L. Zimmerman

THE
PILGRIM
PRESS
Cleveland

Dedicated to
Tom and Mildred,
whose deaths taught me about life

The Pilgrim Press
700 Prospect Avenue
Cleveland, Ohio 44115-1100
thepilgrimpress.com

Printed in the United States of America.

FSC
Mixed Sources
Product group from well-managed
forests and other controlled sources
Cert no. SW-COC-002283
www.fsc.org
© 1996 Forest Stewardship Council

12 11 10 09 08 07   6 5 4 3 2 1

Library of Congress Cataloging-in-Publication Data
Zimmerman, Dennis L., 1953-
   Healing death : finding wholeness when a cure is no longer possible / Dennis L.
Zimmerman.
      p.   cm.
   ISBN 978-0-8298-1760-7 (alk. paper)
   1. Terminally ill – Religious life. 2. Terminally ill. 3. Terminal care. 4. Bereavement –
Religious aspects – Christianity. 5. Death – Religious aspects – Christianity.   I. Title.
BV4910.Z56 2007
248.8′66 – dc22
                                                                        2007000229

Contents

Chapter One

Why Another Book on Death and Dying?

Why do we need another book on death and dying? Isn't there enough written on this sad and painful subject? Why should anyone spend time reading about something people would rather not even think about?

This book grew out of failure and frustration: my own. My sense of failure came from the realization that I had done an absolutely crummy job of being a son to my father when he was dying from cancer. If that was not enough, it also came from my sense of failure at not being able to be of any real help to the families I ministered to as a pastor or chaplain as they faced their own death or the death of a loved one. Sure, I could mouth all the right words. I could pray with and for them. I could perform a meaningful, dignified, and individualized funeral service. But I knew in my heart that I was letting them down. If I was to be a true spiritual leader to them I should know how to be more helpful as they faced this trying time in their lives.

Over time this sense of failure led to a frustrated feeling that someone ought to do something about this. I had met some families who had what it took to truly come together to surround a dying family member with love and support. I had experienced how other families completely fell apart when the added stress of death and dying overwhelmed their ability to cope. But though I could acknowledge a healing experience of death when I saw it, I didn't know how to help a family that wanted to "be there" for their dying loved one but didn't know how. Someone, I thought, ought to write an instruction manual for families on how to love and support a dying loved one in a healthy and healing manner so that when death finally arrived, all those involved — both the person who was dying and the family caregivers — were left feeling they had done their best.

Eventually it became clear to me that if someone was going to do it, it was going to have to be me.

Defining a Healing Death

What follows is a framework for an individual with a chronic, fatal illness *and* a circle of family and friends who will be caring for this individual to live as completely, honestly, and joyfully as they can with whatever time is left to them together. I am not offering a handy blueprint or a simple cookbook recipe for getting through grief. Do not think of this as a do-it-yourself death and dying kit. Think of what follows as more of a paint box giving you the colors you need to paint your own unique grief masterwork.

I am convinced that healing for your mind and soul is always available even when a cure for physical illness is no longer possible. Intentional, well thought out interventions will enable the person who is dying to do so with dignity and peace. Honest and clear-eyed communication and decision making will help surviving loved ones incorporate their losses into the fabric of their hearts, minds, and souls in ways that leave them strengthened and more complete. By taking an active, honest part in coming face to face with the full reality of what is happening, you, both the person who is dying and surviving loved ones, will find that dying is more dignified and serene, that caring is more joyful and sincere, and that your experience of the process is enriched and enhanced.

It is possible to have an experience of death that is healing. *I define a healing death as one in which the person dying and those around him or her come to a point of relative peace and wholeness with themselves and each other about the reality of what is happening.* This doesn't mean that you are happy about dying or watching someone you love die. It doesn't mean that everyone in the family or group of friends involved with the death needs to be at the same emotional place all at the same time. It doesn't mean that everyone expresses grief in the same way or goes through the stages and expressions of grief according to some predetermined formula. The process of death, dying, and grief is more of an art than a science. It is entirely possible — perhaps even likely — that some of those involved will never achieve the same sense of peace that others possess. Still, even if your grief masterwork ends up being less than perfect and some are left with certain unsettled regrets, hurts, and disappointments, it is nonetheless worth the effort to create for yourselves the most beautiful, meaning-filled, and serene experience of death and dying and grief you can.

In a healing death, each person involved is free to honestly experience a sense of loss, and all are able to incorporate the changes death brings into the tapestry of their lives in ways that are personally meaningful. In a healing death, each person has a reasonable sense of confidence in his or her ability to cope with the feelings that accompany death or is willing to get the help he or she needs to cope. In a healing experience of death, each person is willing to trust the others involved and to give them the room they need to approach death in their own individual style. In a healing experience of death, love, support, honesty, and trust take precedence over form, roles, past hurts, expectations, or what someone thinks "should" happen.

One Caveat

One of the assumptions in what follows is that the person who is dying is able to be a part of the give and take of caregiving and receiving. Families dealing with a person who is in a coma or otherwise severely mentally incapacitated may find something useful in what follows, but a lot of what I've written will not apply. Families in which the person who is dying is a child, say preschool or older, will find much that is helpful, but a family facing the approaching death of a newborn may find that what I've written is not exactly what they are looking for.

Getting Started

Someday, maybe sooner than you think, you or someone you love will receive a diagnosis of terminal illness. If you are like most people, you will meet this news with a jumbled mix of emotions — most of them unpleasant. You may feel angry, sad, lied to, abandoned, or confused. You may feel crushed. You may feel frightened. You might even feel a sense of relief that you finally know what is going on. You might feel all of these things at the same time.

Then, if you are like most people, after this first flood of emotion you may find yourself wondering, "What do I do now?" You might be the kind of person who likes to take charge of the situation, to do whatever you can to change it or make it stop. Or you may feel you want to run away and hide. You might feel you can't possibly handle this and look for someone else to take over and tell you what to do. Most of all, you will probably just hope this terrible news will somehow simply go away, that you will wake up and find that it was all just a terrible nightmare, and that all you have to do is take a hot shower and drink a nice cup of tea and it will all disappear like a puff of smoke.

Be assured that these powerful, confusing thoughts and feelings are perfectly natural. Even the most centered, composed, "together" person you can imagine comes unglued when he or she receives news that death is near.

But why? We all know that death is a natural part of life. What makes the news that death is coming soon to you or someone you know so terrifying? Perhaps it is the knowing itself. According to Psalm 8, God has given human beings almost godlike abilities. Among these is the ability to reflect on the past and consider the future. An unpleasant consequence of this wonderful gift of self-awareness, though, is the terrible burden of knowing that all God's children must one day die and that those left behind must face life without their loved ones. The very fact that we can anticipate death is what contributes to its power to frighten us.

So now what? If we have to accept the fact that death is a part of life and that, like it or not, we all can anticipate our own death as well as that of those we love, what do we do with this information? The knowledge that we will die is a two-edged sword. An awareness of mortality can urge us toward a fuller appreciation of the fleeting richness of earthly life. Knowing that our time is limited can impress upon us the need to live each moment to its fullest, to embrace with love those who are nearest and dearest, and to use our gifts and talents in service to God and others before it is too late. Awareness of the reality of death can help us, in the words of Psalm 90, to "gain a heart of wisdom" and therefore enrich and deepen our living.

An awareness of mortality also brings us face to face with our darker, more sinister sides. Knowing that death is inevitable can fill us with dread. Instead of being thankful for what we have, we may become resentful for what we don't have, won't ever have, and may miss out on. Worry about the pain of losing someone can make us reluctant to enter into close, intimate relationships. Anxiety over what may happen as death approaches can lead us to hoard our resources rather than share them with others. Death can become the ultimate enemy against which we struggle in a fruitless attempt to keep the inevitable at bay.

My Story

I am writing these words because I, too, have drunk of that horrible potion of painful emotions and wild thoughts you have just tasted. When I was in my mid-twenties I was fresh out of seminary and serving as pastor at my first church in Fort Wayne, Indiana. With a wife, two small children, house and car payments, and a new career to develop, I was beginning to live my American dream. That's when I got word that my father, who was then in his early fifties, had been diagnosed with cancer of the pancreas. I was sure someone had made some terrible mistake. Dad had always been the picture of health. He jogged four or five miles every day accompanied by his basset hound "Bridget." He had given up cigarettes more than twenty years before. He ate right. He took vitamins. What had he done to deserve this?

Pancreatic cancer was barely treatable in those days. Dad, who had been a pharmacist and so knew more about disease and medication than most people, did everything he was told to do. He took his pills. He ate healthy meals. He continued to exercise as he was able. He even agreed to participate in some experimental drug programs. While the treatments did help some, in the end the cancer spread and he died at the age of fifty-five.

Even though I had made the trip home to see him several times during his illness — we were living in northeastern Indiana and he was in southeastern Ohio — I was totally unprepared for my father to die. I was an ordained Presbyterian minister who had been trained to help others in their times of loss. I had sat and prayed with church members facing death and dying. I had even taken extra training one summer as a chaplain in a coronary intensive care and step-down unit to learn more about how to minister to those who were near death and their families. Still, in spite of all the time I had spent with books, in hospital rooms, and in people's homes, in spite of all I had experienced and learned, my own firsthand experience of the death of someone close to me knocked me to the ground. I had not been able to be helpful when he was sick. I was not much support when he was dying. And then, when he died, I was unable to be any help or comfort to my other family members. I was, in a word, a mess.

Since then I have witnessed many more experiences of loss, both my own and that of parishioners and friends. Working for a while as a hospice chaplain, I had the opportunity to observe, study, and experience more intensely how families face their "walk through the valley of the shadow of death." I was privileged to witness how in some families the blessings of their love for one another and their selflessness toward family members, friends, and even outsiders made their experience of death and dying a thing of beauty. I was also privileged to witness the tragedy of how bitterness and longstanding family resentments and hurts complicated death and dying, making it more painful and scarring than it had to be. I also had time to reflect on my own inability to be helpful when Dad was dying.

What I learned from my experiences as pastor, chaplain, and son is that while at some level we all know that death is a part of life, we do our best to keep such thoughts pushed away, insisting on the fantasy that while death and dying are a part of other people's lives, they will never touch ours. Upon reflection I realized that we do this for good reasons. What kind of life would it be if we spent our every moment awaiting death? I have read excerpts from diaries kept when the bubonic plague (the Black Death) was raging through Europe in the Middle Ages and accounts of the great flu epidemic that ravaged our country during World War I. Death was on everyone's mind. No one knew what caused the disease, how to treat or prevent it, or when they or someone they loved might be snatched away in the middle of the night. Practically every family lost one or more family members. Church hymns and spiritual books written at that time dwelt on the brevity of life and the nearness of eternity. What a grim existence it must have been!

I am writing these words, then, for you — the dying and those who love someone who is dying — in an attempt to provide some hope and direction through a time in your lives you would rather not go through but find yourself smack in the middle of. What follows is both a theoretical framework to help you address death and dying and practical advice and solid suggestions with which you and those you love can come together to build your own, unique, custom-fit plan to find healing when a cure is no longer possible.

Two Parties Involved

In what follows I am going to be working on the assumption that there are two parties involved in this experience of death and dying: the person who is dying and the cluster of family and friends who are committed to serve as caregivers who will be helping the dying person to die with dignity and peace. Each of these parties has an important role to play. The person who is dying will be the primary player. It is this person's wishes and comfort that will take primary importance. The role of the others is to form a loving, honest, mutually supportive community that will enable the dying person's final months, weeks, and days to be as healing as possible.

The reason for addressing both parties in one book is that it has been my experience that the dying and those who will be caring for them share many of the same questions and anxieties. The problem is that neither knows how to talk with the other about it. More than that, both also tend to want to "spare" the other from the sorrow and suffering that thinking about death and dying brings. As a result, both the dying and those who care for them often feel they must tiptoe around, trying not to "upset" the other — as if crying or feeling sad were some sort of crime.

But this polite dance of hide-and-seek almost never works. Thoughts and feelings slip out. A tear drops before it can be surreptitiously wiped away. Snatches of phone conversations are overheard. Family members hem and haw and try to decide if this is "the right time to talk about it." Brave, if phony, smiles are plastered on faces. And before they know it their very attempts to be polite have locked them into positions where *no one* feels they can talk and *everyone* ends up feeling frustrated and unsatisfied.

As I write about this now, from the vantage point of not currently being caught up in the emotion of an impending death, it all seems so obvious to me. How silly it is to try to hide our emotions at a time of death and dying! If there is ever a time in life to be upset, it is when you are facing death. You are dying! You are about to lose a dearly loved person! If the time of death and dying is not the time for crying or feeling sad, when is? We are *supposed* to be upset in the face of death and there is no shame in letting others know how upset we are!

It is my belief that this reluctance to be honest and open with one another in the face of the terrible reality of approaching death contributes to the suffering of the dying and those who love them rather than reducing it. The very act of hiding our thoughts and feelings from one another — and from ourselves — keeps us from the intimacy we crave and need at this critical moment in life.

Some of you may be facing death in a home setting, perhaps with the help of hospice or other medical professionals. Some of you may be trying to handle it all on your own without professional help. Some of you may be using a care facility (nursing home, hospice house, etc.) or some other professional setting. Whatever the setting you are in as you address the approach of death, it is important for the dying and for caregivers to be able to express their thoughts and feelings with one another in ways that are helpful and healing. Both the dying and those who love them must have permission to be their honest selves while allowing the others to be their honest selves as well.

It is my hope that these few pages might provide a way for both of you, the dying and those who love them, to identify your thoughts and feelings about death and dying. Further, it is my hope that this book will provide you with ways to talk with those around you about what is really important at this most poignant transition point in your lives.

How to Use This Book

This book is part theoretical framework to help you think about your healing experience of death and part practical workbook to help you actually create that experience. Chapters 1, 2, and 3 contain some introductory remarks. This will give you some of my background and experience in this subject so you can see where I'm coming from. You will also find some initial thoughts for caregivers and care receivers.

Chapter 4 is an introduction to grief. Grief is the complex "stew" of emotions and thoughts that tends to render even the most competent of us helpless in the face of death and dying. By recognizing the power and the different faces of grief you will be better enabled to work with and through your grief rather than have it control you.

In chapter 6, you will find a plan for finding healing when a cure is no longer possible. I list eight strategies whereby both the dying and their loved ones can work their way through the process of dying in such a way as to find wholeness as individuals and as a family so that when the moment of separation comes it can be an occasion for celebration and letting go.

In chapter 8, I offer help for families who discover that the goal of finding healing in the face of death is far more difficult than first imagined. Here I introduce some concepts from Family Systems Theory that will help you understand why so many of us find it so hard to work openly and honestly with the people we are closest to. Family Systems Theory offers a no-fault way for family members to recognize the "dysfunctional" dynamics that keep them from working together and suggests ways to replace these unhelpful dynamics with more useful ones.

Chapters 5, 7, and 9 are the practical parts of this book. In these chapters I provide a list of questions designed to help you think through the issues raised in the previous chapter. To get the most use from these "issues" chapters, I encourage you to get a notebook in which you can jot down your answers. If there are more than one of you working through this book you could use the same notebook, or you might consider separate notebooks. If you decide to go the separate route, I encourage you to exchange notebooks and read each other's answers. This will help you start to build the communication process that is an essential part of what you are trying to do. Also, leave plenty of room to go back and add additional thoughts, insights, and information as they come to you.

Appendixes A, B, and C offer resources for creating a funeral or memorial service. Some people may think it sounds a little macabre to plan a funeral before you are dead. But what better way to make sure your send-off is uniquely yours than to have a hand in deciding what will be said and done?

Finally, before you plunge into the work itself I want to thank you for trusting me to guide you during this most intimate of life's journeys. Dying, in spite of all the medical gadgetry and technological sophistication involved, is still a very personal and private experience. I am honored you would invite me into your circle of advisors.

Chapter Two

To the Person Who Is Dying

Birds do it, bees do it, even educated fleas do it...

You know what I'm talking about: kick the bucket, buy the farm, decease, expire, go to heaven, go to a better place, go "home," go to live with (1) God, (2) your Maker, (3) the angels, pass on, croak, fold your tent, pass away, go to Davy Jones's locker, stop breathing, succumb, lose the fight, lose the battle, leave this world, be no longer with us, pass over, go to the great _____ in the sky, be at the last roundup, sleep forever, flat-line, sleep eternally, push up daisies, be six feet under, be at peace, cross over, be worm food, be underground, be asleep, be beneath the sod/waves, be disposed of, have your candle burn out, have your heart/lungs/kidneys/etc. fail, say your last goodbye, make your final exit, fade away, be knockin' on heaven's door. Or, to use just plain English: die.

It is amazing the number of ways we have to *not* talk about something that is going to happen to every one of us. Some of these sayings are folksy and humorous. Some are pious and religious. Some are coldly medicinal. Some even sound vaguely accusatory, as if it was your fault that you died. But the reality is that none of us gets out of life alive.

The Difference between Death and Dying

When I think of death and dying I see these as two different, though certainly related things. The difference between them is the difference between a noun and a verb, a destination and a journey,

Death is a state of being. Death is a noun, a destination. Some people worry a lot about what happens to them when they die. I don't, for the simple reason that what happens after I am dead is out of my hands. As I see it, one of two things happens to us when we are dead.

One possibility is that dead is dead: that when we die we cease to exist in any form whatsoever. The elements of which we are composed — carbon, oxygen, hydrogen, nitrogen, iron, and a host of trace elements — are all recycled into the soil, where they are used to build new forms of life. Any sense of our spiritual or mental existence — what religious people call a "soul" — if it ever existed, dissipates into the great beyond and the only thing left behind is memories in some other person's mind.

If this is what happens when we are dead, there is nothing to worry about. If life is nothing more than the accidental meeting of the right numbers of atoms in the right configuration, then the end of life is nothing more than the redistribution of those elements. There is no eternal reward. There is no eternal punishment. We are truly nothing more than "worm food" in the best sense of that phrase. Though some people find this thought reassuring, I personally find this possibility a bit depressing. Perhaps it is just ego speaking, but I like to think that I am something more than a pile of chemicals and that something of "me" will exist after I am dead.

The other possibility is that dead is not dead or at least not completely dead; that when we die our body returns to the earth, but our spirit — our eternal life force — continues in some form. I am familiar with two ways of understanding eternal existence. The first is a sort of eternal existence that is not really eternal life. According to this understanding, even though our life force continues on, our individuality, our particular essence or personality, ends when our earthly life ends and the goal of eternal being is *nirvana*, a kind of spiritual existence with no existence; a reabsorption of individuality back into the primordial spark of life.

Another understanding of eternal existence is that our spirit or soul continues in some recognizable form in what Christians and some others call "eternal life." The concept of eternal life is that not only our spark of life but our individuality continues in an identifiable form. The Bible, the source Christians turn to for information on this concept of eternal life, is a bit vague on the particulars, but we get several hints. The Bible talks about "those who are asleep in the Lord" being "caught up with him in the clouds" (1 Thessalonians). The Bible talks about Jesus going to prepare a "home" for us within his "mansion" (John 14). St. Paul writes to the Corinthian church about the necessity for the perishable to put on imperishability and for the mortal to put on immortality (1 Corinthians 15). Paul also asserts that if there is a physical body there is certainly a spiritual body (1 Corinthians 15).

What does all this mean, exactly? I have to confess that I don't know, exactly.

As I am writing this my almost-two-year-old grandson, Eben, is learning English. My wife, who is a speech therapist, tells me he has good vocalization ability and that he has a large vocabulary for his age. (But then, isn't everyone's grandchild the smartest and cutest of them all?) What he hasn't quite figured out yet, though, is what words go with what objects. The other day he learned the word "monkey." For the next several days every animal — dogs, cats, squirrels, etc. — was "monkey." All wheeled objects have been "car-car" for months, even the trucks. Eben is learning that words describe certain realities, even though he is not 100 percent clear how the words and the realities go together.

In the same way I am convinced that what the Bible has to say about soul, spirit, spiritual body, being with God, and eternal life all describe something that is real even though I don't know exactly how that reality operates. I am content that in some marvelous way that is beyond my complete understanding God has taken care of the details of "dead" so that I don't have to worry about them. I am certain that "dead" will be a place of continuing existence and individuality where I will know "as I "have been known" (1 Corinthians 13) and where I will continue to be in eternal relationship with those who have died before me.

But...if I am content with the realities of "death" and "dead," I am *much* less confident and comfortable with the idea of dying. Dying is the active part of the question. Dying is the verb, the journey. Dying is what happens on this side of the grave.

If death is *beyond* our control, dying is very much *in* our control. The whole medical-industrial complex is a multi-billion-dollar enterprise that revolves around trying to control dying in its various forms and guises. As I consider my own dying I am aware that there are many things to worry about. Will I be in pain? Will I suffer? Will I be surrounded by those who love me? Will I be abandoned and left all alone? Will I be in my right mind? Will I spend weeks, months, or years disabled in some way? Will my final disease or accident leave my body disfigured? Will my wishes for my body and my possessions be carried out? Will I be remembered with love and affection or will I be remembered with indifference? Will I be bed-bound? Will I have the chance to say goodbye to those I love? Will I be able to reconcile with those with whom I have had differences? Will I have an opportunity to apologize to those I have harmed? How much time do I have left? How will the people I love get by without me here? Will the people I love get along without me better than I think they will? What if no one misses me? What am I going to miss out on if I die sooner than I want to? Will I die suddenly, or over a long period of time? Will my dying be a physical, emotional, or financial hardship on others? Will someone have to change my dirty diapers? Will I be able to do all the things I want to do before I die or will I be too sick and feeble to do them? Will I be an object of pity or scorn or ridicule?

Yes, for my money dead is a piece of cake. Either there is a God who is waiting to welcome me into his eternal arms or there is the great silence of the eternal void. It is dying that causes me to lose sleep. And as I face all the issues and worries that swirl in my mind as I contemplate my dying I am left with one other question: Is there anything I can do about any of these things?

There is actually good news on the dying front. Never in the history of the world have there been as many aids to dying as there are today, and new ways of making dying easier and less trying are being developed every day. Medical science has advanced tremendously in the last hundred years and the pace of medical discovery is rapidly increasing. When I was a child, a diagnosis of cancer was a certain death sentence. Now many forms of cancer are completely curable and other forms can be treated so that many years of pain-free and relatively unencumbered life can be enjoyed even though the cancer continues. HIV/AIDS was once a thief in the night snatching the life from those who contracted it. Now, with new medications available, people are living decades with the virus under control.

Not only has medical care improved, but so have nursing homes and other care facilities. Sure, you still hear about certain "hell hole" nursing homes where people are not looked after properly, but for the most part things are much better now than they were even just a few years ago. The hospice movement has made dying much more humane and much less frightening as teams of medical personnel, social workers, and chaplains who are specialists in dying are now available to help both the dying person and that person's family and friends as they go through the dying process.

Yet a third way that dying is much less terrifying than it was in past years is the development of a new attitude among the dying themselves. In the past one was a victim of dying. Because medical science knew so little about the causes of death and could do so little about the causes it did know about, dying was perceived to be a passive thing. The person who was dying could do little more than lie back and take it.

Now, however, the dying are invited and even expected to take an active part in what is happening to them. Where once the dying were passive victims, they are now seen as active participants. The dying are now part of the team that decides how and where and to some degree when the dying is going to take place.

Taking Charge of Your Own Dying

This book is a tool to help you take charge of your dying process. In the pages that follow, you and your care team of family and friends will be stating your wishes and making plans for making your experience of dying as comfortable, peaceful, and healing as possible.

If this is going to happen, it is going to take some major input from you. If you were the one who bought this book, I salute you. You have decided that you are not going to go "quietly into the night," but are going to take an active part in your final days no matter how many or how few they may be. It is now up to you to gather friends and family to begin to put your plan together.

If someone else has bought this book and is now asking you to work with him or her to create a healing environment for your death, you should feel humbled, for you are indeed blessed. Someone loves you enough to want to plan to make your final days as comfortable as possible and to see that your wishes for the end of your life are carried out.

In either case the work set before you is going to be tough. This is no task for sissies! There are four things in particular that you need to do to make this process of finding healing in death work.

First, you are going to have to be honest both with yourself and with the others. This is no time for false modesty or deathbed bravado. State your wishes clearly. Now is not the time to worry about what is "realistic" or what is "too much trouble." Now is the time to describe what you want done and why. Most, perhaps almost all of what you want to happen will certainly happen. In all likelihood not every one of your wishes will be met exactly as you would like. But not letting others know what is in your heart will guarantee that your desires will never be met.

Second, you need to be kind. If dying is hard for you, so is it for those around you. You are faced with losing your life. They are faced with losing someone they love. Your pain and suffering will soon be over. Theirs is just beginning. If at first others are reluctant to engage with you in conversation about dying, don't press too hard. Give them a chance to warm up to the idea. We live in a "death-denying" culture. We Americans live with the false belief that we can buy our way out of any situation. It may take the others a while to realize that you are serious about handling dying in a direct and open manner before they are willing or able to join in with you.

Third, you need to not die until you are actually dead. Though you may want to crawl into your bed and pull the covers over your head, this is not the time to run and hide. Your caregivers need you to give them instructions on how you want your dying to unfold. Even though they love you very much, your caregivers cannot read your mind. They need you to tell them when what they are doing isn't working and when something needs to change. There may come a time when you are ready to stop trying. That will be your prerogative and you will know when that time has arrived. Right now, though, is not that time.

And finally, you need to trust. Trust yourself — that you are able to face dying with honesty and with grace. Trust the others — that they will be there for you and will do their best to make you as comfortable and loved as they are able. Trust the process — that there is an orderly and dignified way to die and that death can be the ultimate healing. And, if it is your belief, trust God — that there is a place prepared for you and that he will take you home to be with him.

Chapter Three

To the Caregivers

I have not even met you and yet I already like and admire you. You are about to give someone the greatest gift imaginable: the gift of a loving and healing death. You may be facing this task with an inner calm and composure. You may be full of worries and doubts about your ability to pull it off. You may be doing this as an act of love or as an act of obligation. You may be doing this as part of a team of family members and friends or you may be about to try to do this all on your own. You may have great insurance and excellent medical assistance. You may be trying to get by on modest resources. Whatever your particular situation, the very fact that you are starting down this road tells me that you are a person of courage and generous spirit. Thank you for giving of both.

Our Changing Times

In some ways caring for the dying is not such a new thing. People have been caring for their dying loved ones for as long as there have been people and loved ones. But we are living in a particular time and place in history when the idea of family and friends doing hands-on care for a dying loved one is seen as something of a novelty.

Prior to World War I, medical care in the United States was rudimentary at best. In fact, when World War I began medicine had improved only slightly from what was practiced during the American Civil War. Admission to medical schools was open to practically anyone who could pay the tuition regardless of undergraduate preparation or grades. There was little uniformity in training and few standards of care. There were no miracle drugs. There were only a few painkillers, and these were often poorly understood and poorly administered. Doctors had little more to offer patients than the most primitive of surgical procedures (before which they may or may not have washed their hands and instruments), herbs and ointments largely passed down from folk medicine, and perhaps a bit of human kindness and sympathy.

After World War I, and especially after World War II, however, all of this changed. World War I and the great influenza epidemic of 1918 ushered in a new urgency for improvements in medical care. The uncontrolled dying of thousands of people as war and flu circled the globe shocked people and spurred on the first systematic application of scientific thinking to the practice of medicine. The results of this systematic, scientific thinking were nothing less than phenomenal. For the first time in history doctors could be expected to treat, cure, and even prevent diseases that had plagued humanity for hundreds of years. This was the era that brought us vaccines, sterile surgery, antibiotics, and chemotherapy. This was the era that brought standardization to the practice of medicine and to admission to and graduation from medical schools. Hospitals changed from being places you went to die to places you went expecting to be treated and released.

A funny thing happened to American culture, though, during these heady and exciting days when the promises of medical miracles seemed endless. Somehow people got to thinking that doctors could cure anything, and doctors did little to correct this mistaken idea. These days of "better living" through the application of science, technology, and chemistry lured us into thinking that, given the right medical team, the proper diagnosis, and the appropriate treatment, we could live forever. Death was the enemy. Death was no longer seen as a normal part of life but as a "failure" on the part of the doctors for not doing the right thing or of the patient for not getting better. What had always been a natural phenomenon became an embarrassment.

Prior to World War I, relatively few people ever left the hospital alive. In fact, most people never went to the hospital at all, but stayed at home and were looked after by friends, family, and neighbors. What little medical attention they received was administered by doctors who came to their homes. When they died they were laid out in the family home and often buried on the family property. Death and dying were an unpleasant, though natural, part of every family's experience. Undertakers were contracted to provide a coffin, a hearse, and perhaps a few other burial services, but most of the work of preparation and actual burial was done by the family with help from neighbors and church friends.

Between the beginning of the First World War and the end of the Second World War, death and dying were removed from the hands of family, friends, and neighbors and handed over to professionals. Few people died at home any more. Most died in sterile white hospital wards, often alone, often either in pain or oversedated. This was not because people no longer cared. This was the "modern" way of handling death. Family members, no matter how well-intended, were seen as being incapable of handling the dying process and needed to be kept away. Similarly, it was understood that it took a professional to properly "dispose" of the body once someone died. Undertakers became funeral directors, and funeral homes were now thought of as the proper place for the visitation of a deceased loved one. Again, family and friends were shunted to the side to allow for a more proper and "expert" handling of the situation.

We now find ourselves in a new situation, influenced by the last several years but somehow different. Medical treatment is almost never done at home anymore. Hospitals are still considered places where medical miracles happen, but we also know that not everyone who goes to the hospital lives to tell about it. Medical professionals are still respected for their knowledge and their skill but they are much less revered as the gods of science they were once considered to be. Though many more treatments are available to bring relief and even cure to many more conditions, we are beginning to come to terms with the reality that death is not so much the enemy as it is a part of life. As for the funeral services, I don't ever expect to see the day when viewings and funerals are held in private homes again, but I am impressed with the new flexibility I see from funeral directors and their willingness to let families have a larger say in customizing what they want done.

If medical personnel, funeral personnel, and families are starting to come to the realization that we need a less institutional, more personal and human way of dealing with the reality of death and dying, perhaps the greatest innovation in the care of the dying to come about in recent years has been the rise of hospice care. The dedicated men and women of the hospice movement are skilled professionals who understand the complexity of dying. They are not afraid of the emotional messiness. And, most important of all in my opinion, they are trained to work with the dying and with family caregivers and to let them take the lead in making critical decisions about how and where dying will take place.

The Caregiver's Part in the Dying Process

If you have not already read chapter 2, "To the Person Who Is Dying," please do so. There I said that it is the dying person who is in charge of the dying process. The caregiver's job is to help carry out the dying person's wishes to the best of your ability. This doesn't mean that anything goes, of course. What it does mean is that there needs to be a partnership between the person who is dying and those who will be doing the caregiving. By and large, your job is going to be to manage the day-to-day care of your dying loved one according to the plan and following the wishes that have been laid out. For some people this will mean regular visits to the care facility where the dying person resides. For others it will mean moving into your loved one's home or having your loved one move into your home for a period of time. Some families will opt for hands-on care. Other families will use paid professionals. Chances are, if your loved one chooses to die at home, you will end up with a combination of personal and professional caregiving. For some families, then, it will be physical care that will dominate the picture. For others the emotional transitions will be the most trying. For yet others, family dysfunction will place particular challenges before them.

Though it is your dying loved one who is the primary player in the dying process, the rest of this book is designed to help you be with them through death and beyond. Here we will discuss the kinds of things families used to do to ease dying before we developed all our scientific attempts to keep death hidden away. Even if it was your dying loved one who bought this book, initiated the process, and has already started to answer many of the questions at the end of each of the following chapters, it is going to fall to you who are caregivers to follow this process through to the end.

I have suggested above four specific things that the dying person must do to make this process work: be honest with self and others; be kind to self and others; not give up too soon; and trust in self, others, the process, and God. Caregivers would do well to do these four things as well. In addition, I am going to suggest that there are four things to which caregivers need to pay particular attention.

First, keep your perspective. Being with a dying loved one means being intimately connected with thoughts and feelings that can become over-whelming. You will see and smell and experience things that will test you physically, emotionally, and spiritually. You need to have some way of stepping out of the situation, if only in your mind. Even though you may have opted for complete, in-home, hands-on care, I encourage you to re-serve some corner of your life as your own. Your own mental and spiritual health is important. Even though time may be scarce, continue with hob-bies, pastimes, and people you enjoy. Stay connected to the things and relationships that give you pleasure and a sense of meaning. This time of caregiving, as precious and intense a gift as it is, will come to an end. You need to have a life to return to.

Second, take physical care of yourself. This is particularly important for caregivers who are themselves elderly or have ongoing health issues. I have seen too many caregivers who have become so worn out with taking care of someone else that their own health and well-being deteriorates until they are no longer able to care for their loved one. Take advantage of the visits of others to slip away, even if only for a short while. Watch your diet and make sure you are getting the nutrition you need. Make sure you are doing what you can to get a good night's sleep. Shower. Brush your teeth. Comb your hair. Remember Jesus' teaching that it is just as important to love ourselves as it is to love others.

Third, remember to be human. You are not a superhero, even though you might like to be. Neither are you a doormat, as much as you might feel like one from time to time. You have limitations and you have abilities. Have a sense of them both. Know when to say no and when to say yes. Remember that the most important line in the old Alcoholics Anonymous prayer is this: the wisdom to know the difference.

Finally, keep breathing. There will be times when you will feel the weight of the world crushing you. There will be times when it will feel as if all the air has been sucked out of the room. In both situations, keep breathing. Remember one of the other bits of wisdom AA members have discovered: One Day at a Time. Sometimes it is one hour at a time. Sometimes it is one breath at a time. But whatever you do, keep breathing.

A Note on the Use of Humor

If you have not already noticed, even though I regard death and dying as a terribly serious topic, I like to throw a little humor into the discussion from time to time. Please don't think I am making fun of you or your situation. It is just my way of cutting some of the tension this topic can cause. If you find it offensive or distracting, please overlook it and accept my apology.

Chapter Four

Facing the Unpleasant Reality of Death and Grief

Death Is Real

Of all the issues we will ever face in our lives, coming to grips with the reality of death is the hardest. Death is permanent. Death is final. Death is often painful. Death causes suffering. Death is shrouded in uncertainty, pain, fear, loss, and a whirlwind of other hard, unpleasant emotions. While there are some people who have been able to process the reality of death so that it has lost some of its power to alarm, death challenges most of us by upsetting our emotional, spiritual, and social equilibrium and bringing us face to face with issues we would rather avoid.

Try as we may, we cannot escape the fact of death. Neither can we shield ourselves — or others — from the certainty that sooner or later we, they, or someone dearly loved will come to the end of his or her life on earth. And when the specter of death draws near, as it surely will, we have but one choice: to incorporate the changes death brings to our lives as best we can.

The first time one faces the reality of death and dying is usually the worst. If this is your first experience of the death of someone close to you, hang in there. Though you may feel you can't handle this, you have more resources at your command than you may think. Although you may never have had to deal with the death of a close friend or family member before, you have certainly experienced loss in one form or another. Loss is a friend moving away. Loss is leaving your beloved grade school and making the move up to that big, scary junior high. Loss is leaving home. Loss is the death of a pet or even a plant. Loss is living in the empty nest when all your children have flown the coop. As painful as each of these experiences has been, each experience of loss has prepared you for this time of ultimate loss. Each of these losses has exercised your emotional, spiritual, and intellectual "muscles," making you strong in the face of your loss. You can now draw on that strength as you face this trying moment.

Healing Is Not the Same as Curing

Before we go any further I want to explain the terms we are going to use to describe the experience of death and dying. I want to do this because the very words we use to describe our experience have the power to frame that experience and fill it with meaning. Specifically, I want to look at the words "healing" and "curing."

Most people use the words "heal" and "cure" to mean the same thing. But though they may be interchangeable in everyday conversation they actually have two very different meanings.

"Cure" comes from a Latin root relating to both "trouble" and "managing." Over time, "cure" came to mean the management of trouble or the fixing of problems. One problem people had to face before the era of our modern electrical conveniences was the preservation of food so that it would not spoil. Salting or smoking food in such a way as to draw out moisture and thus keep it from bacterial decay became known as "curing" it. Oddly enough, over time the use of "curing" also became a way to describe the management or fixing of medical and physical ailments; the "preservation" of life if you will. To "cure" a disease is to find a medical remedy, to "fix it." To "cure" someone is to preserve that person from death.

"Heal," on the other hand, comes from an Old English word meaning "whole" or "healthy." Its root meaning relates to the forming of new skin over a wound, making complete once again what was torn. "Healing" also relates to spiritual and emotional wholeness, and it is primarily in this sense that I use the word here. "Heal," "healthy," "whole," and "holy" all have a common root.

It is my belief that healing is possible even when a cure is not. One can find wholeness and holiness in the experience of death and dying even after the best doctors in the world have had to admit there is nothing else they can do to bring about a cure. A "healing death" is my way of describing a death in which spiritual and emotional wholeness is formed, preserved, enhanced, and celebrated even as the physical body deteriorates. I believe it is possible to heal the spirit, to restore relationships, and to find wholeness in life even as death draws near.

Pain and Suffering Are Not the Same

Let's look at one other pair of words often associated with death and dying. We speak of the "pain of death." In almost the same breath we also talk about the "suffering" of those who are dying and of those who love them. I want to suggest to you that "pain" and "suffering" are not the same.

"Pain," as I am using it here, refers to physical pain. There is often a lot of pain associated with death and dying. Cancer hurts. Emphysema hurts. Heart disease can be excruciating. Thanks be to God, though, that we live in an era when we no longer have to simply lie there and endure physical pain. We live in a time of tremendous advances in pain relief. Some doctors actually specialize in pain relief in a practice known as "palliative care."

If the person who is dying is experiencing pain, talk to your doctor. If you are not offered the relief you want, ask to speak to a palliative care specialist. They are often associated with the oncology (cancer) department, but will generally be available to help you even if you are not dealing with cancer.

"But," you may be asking, "what about emotional hurt? Doesn't that count as pain?" Of course, emotional hurt in painful. Anyone who has ever had his or her heart broken knows that the pain of emotional hurt is real. However, what is sometimes called emotional hurt or pain I am going to call by another name: "suffering."

Suffering is emotional and/or spiritual pain.

Not all physical pain causes suffering. For example, I love to work on things around the house and to tinker with minor repairs on the car. I like to consider myself something of a handyman. The only problem is that every time I pick up a tool to work on something I cut myself. I am the only person I know who can cut himself on a hammer! When I cut myself, it hurts. It bleeds. It is annoying. I have to stop what I'm doing and get a bandage so I don't get blood all over whatever I'm working on. But it doesn't rock my world — unless, of course, I *really* hurt myself, which I have been known to do. Generally, though, I don't go into an emotional tailspin over a little torn skin, the loss of a few drops of blood, and a few minutes of overstimulated nerve endings — though I will confess to sometimes saying a few words I would not want my congregation to hear me say.

Suffering occurs when hurt and pain lead to emotional and spiritual uncertainty — what theologians call "ontological angst" (there will be a vocabulary test later!). If my little handyman incident had threatened the loss of life or limb or seriously disrupted my life so that it caused me to wonder about my future ability to provide for my family, it would have crossed the line from pain to suffering. Or consider the many times we hear about floods or famines or earthquakes or other human tragedies in other parts of the world. Often we are moved to pray for the people affected and may even donate to a relief fund. But except for cases of extraordinary loss of life like the tsunami that struck parts of Asia in January of 2006 or the hurricanes that came onshore along the Gulf Coast of the United States that same year, or unless we, our family, or someone we know is directly involved, the pain of others generally doesn't keep us up at night. What turns pain into suffering is that we feel a personal connection to the events or the people involved in the event.

If, as I am suggesting, it is true that not all physical pain leads to suffering, it is possible to suffer even though we experience no physical pain at all. I remember when my children were young and they were going through all those lovely "learning experiences" we all have to endure in the process of growing up, almost all of them painful. You remember them:

a best friend who doesn't want to play any more, a heartbreaking loss at a sports event, an embarrassing mistake on stage, a budding romance that falls apart, a teacher or classmate who is making life unbearable. I remember how my heart would ache, knowing that my children were going through a bad time and there was nothing I could do to make things better for them. My child was the one going through pain but, because of my emotional links to my child, I was experiencing suffering even though nothing pain-causing had happened directly to me.

As I noted above, medical science often is able to bring relief for the physical pain of dying. But medical science can't do diddly (please excuse my technical language) for emotional or spiritual suffering. You definitely want to take advantage of any and all medications, massages, or any other means of comfort you are offered when you are in physical pain. Also, some persons may temporarily need to take a tranquilizer of some sort to help them with the emotional shock of what they are going through. But we should not want to be so sedated on medication that we are unable to enjoy the presence of family and friends as we pass from life to death.

However, surgery, medication, massage, or other means of pain relief cannot relieve suffering. To handle suffering you have turn to other forms of treatment: love, a sense of humor, prayer, honest conversation, emotional release (screaming, crying, laughing, shouting, etc.), being grateful, giving of yourself. Have you ever thought of love as a treatment for suffering? Have you ever considered setting aside the aspirins and taking two jokes before calling in the morning? Had any good heart-to-hearts with God lately?

Grief Is Real

We call the suffering that accompanies death — or any loss for that matter — "grief." Grief is a time of adjustment and change. It is a time of letting go and starting up. In fact, this adjusting and changing, letting go and starting up, is one of the things that makes grief so difficult. After all, if we were to be truly honest about it, most of us don't like change. We especially don't like change when it is forced upon us. Speaking for myself — and perhaps you, too — I don't like the sense of being out of control that forced change brings. But like it or not, the changes brought on by grief are an intricate, unavoidable part of death and dying.

Grief is unavoidable because death is unavoidable. This unavoidability is another factor that complicates dealing with grief. Let's face it, most of us don't like to dwell on life's problems. We can, if we work at it, avoid many of life's unpleasant issues, at least temporarily. Many of life's setbacks can be ignored, at least for a while. For example, who hasn't tried to overlook that "funny sound" coming from under the car, hoping it will just go away? Or have you ever had to get up and walk away from a table full of bills and a checkbook short of money, hoping that a miraculous windfall will suddenly occur and make the whole problem go away? Have you ever had something really important to say to someone, but you just can't seem to find the right time or place to say it?

You can't do any of this with death. Death refuses to be ignored or set aside. If you are the one left behind, there is no way you can miss the empty place at the dinner table, the pillow that goes unused, the voice you no longer hear, the hand that no longer reaches for yours. If you are the one dying, there comes a time when you can no longer deny your weakening condition, your increasing reliance on others, your sense that the end may be near. Death is real and cannot be overlooked. Grief happens, and there is nothing we can do to stop it.

Different Styles of Grieving

Contrary to popular myth, there is no "right" way to grieve. Each of us brings our personality, experiences, understanding, and beliefs to bear in creating our own individual expression of grief. I remember one couple I worked with after their son died. They came to me initially because they were considering divorce — an all-too-common complication of the death of a child — and wanted someone to try to help them work things out.

The mother was grieving very openly and publicly. She carried pictures of her son with her all the time. She attended two or three grief support groups a week. She could easily talk about her sense of loss and readily relied on her many friends for comfort and support.

The father, in contrast, was grieving very privately. Like many men, he did not have the emotional vocabulary his wife had. It wasn't that he didn't feel the loss. He simply didn't have the words to express what he was feeling. Neither did his circle of friends have the expertise to listen to and process grief that his wife and her friends had. He resisted her repeated invitations to attend grief support groups because he found them too uncomfortable. "Just a bunch of people sitting around crying" is how he described them. He seldom talked about their son with his wife. When he got together with his friends, he talked about golf.

"See what I mean," the mother would angrily say to me. "He never loved our son. How can he just go on as if nothing has happened? How can I stay married to a man like him?"

"Why does she keep needling me about this?" the father would ask. "I loved Jimmy as much as or more than she did. Why can't she just let it go?"

As we worked together over the next several weeks, they were able to see that both of them had loved their son very much and that both of them missed him deeply. They were both expressing their grief in the only way they knew how. Their problem was that they were each expecting the other to express grief exactly as they did. As they learned to relax and give each other permission to be themselves, they reconciled and decided not to get divorced after all.

As this dramatic example points out, some people grieve quietly and stoically and some people grieve openly and loudly. Some people are very private with their grief. They keep their upper lip very stiff. They shed not a tear — at least not in pubic. Other people are more demonstrative. They weep publicly. They talk about what is bothering them.

Neither style is better or worse than the other. Neither is a more correct or a less correct way to grieve. They are different; that's all. It is important for a family or group of friends who will be experiencing loss and grief together to recognize that they will not all be grieving exactly alike, and they will need to have enough grace and tolerance among themselves to make room for each person's expression of loss.

I sometimes hear family members trying to predict how they or others will handle grief. They are almost always wrong. It has been my experience that, though we may think we know someone well, a profound experience of deep personal loss may lead that person to react in ways we had not expected. In the example I used above, it was the mother who grieved publicly and the father who grieved privately. The roles can easily be reversed.

I have a friend, a retired army chaplain, who has seen combat and has witnessed the death of many fine young men — and women — in horrifying circumstances. But when his daughter was killed when a drunk driver crossed the center line and ran head on into her car, this tough, battle-hardened man had to be sedated to get through her funeral. Fifteen years later he still teared up at the memory of her death.

At the other extreme, I have seen more than one "delicate" person, who everyone thought would never be able to handle a stressful loss, become the one the others leaned on for support. I have been amazed at how often it is the dying person who becomes the support person for those who will be left to go on.

In short, if there is one thing I can say about diversity in grieving style, it is this: *be flexible*. Be flexible with yourself and with others. Grief pushes each of us in unexpected ways. You may be surprised to find that one day you can't stop talking about what you are feeling even though you are usually quiet and reserved. Or, by contrast, you may reach the point where you don't even want to think about it, let alone talk about it, even though you are usually quite expressive about your feelings. The same thing goes for other family members and friends. Sometimes people need to talk. Sometimes people just want to be left alone.

Ideally, you and your loved ones will develop a sense of rhythm with one another and create a sense that it is permissible to talk or not talk as you feel the need. I encourage you to feel free to take turns being expressive or quiet. Give yourself and each other permission to "be strong" and to "fall apart." If you are really brave, try intentionally expressing your grief in a way contrary to your natural inclinations. If you are naturally a talker, try being quiet. If you are naturally someone who tends to keep things inside, try expressing yourself more openly. You might be surprised to find out just how strong or tender you and the others might actually be.

Children and Grief

Adults are often at a loss when it comes to knowing how to talk with children about death and dying. In general, I would encourage you to be as honest with children about what is happening as possible. Give them as much information as they are able to accept at that time. Take their questions seriously, but don't try to overload them with more than they can handle.

Child development experts tell us that young children's minds are not able to handle such abstract concepts as life, death, or afterlife. In fact, it is not until children are in high school — say fourteen or fifteen years old — that they are really able to grasp the eternal mysteries of death. Young children will tend to take what we say about death and dying literally, so we have to be very careful how we explain things "on their level." For example, one family told their six-year-old that "Grandpa was getting ready to sleep with the angels." That sounds like a lovely, gentle thing to say to a child. In fact though, such poetic euphemisms are really a way to make the adults feel better. For the child they just cause more confusion in what is already a puzzling situation. These parents thought they had done a good job explaining things until, over the next several days, their six-year-old began to stump them with a whole new series of questions:

"When will Grandpa be waking up?"

"Why do the angels want to take Grandpa away?"

"If I fall asleep, will the angels take me away, too?"

"What are the angels going to do with Grandpa when they get him?"

Obviously, their attempt to "break it to her gently" had just complicated matters and had given her a whole new set of things to worry about.

It is better that you go ahead and use the words "death" and "dying" rather than try to cover up what is going on with some clever folksy way of talking around it. Will children be frightened if you use words like "death" or "dying"? They might be, but this is where your job really begins. Words like "death," "dying," "terminal illness," "passing away," and the like evoke a strong emotional response from adults because we associate them with loss and emotional suffering. We know what it is like to lose someone to death. Our job as adults is to introduce these words to our children in a way that helps them know that death and dying are real but also in a way that enables them to incorporate this reality into their lives with a minimum of fear.

Adults need to be adult when talking to children about death and dying. If you talk with your children about death and dying only in an emotional climate of fear and upset, your children will associate these concepts with fear and upset. If you talk with them about death and dying in a calm and accepting mood, your children will begin to understand that they are a normal part of life. Even though their minds may not be able to conceive of all the abstract subtleties these words contain, they will pick up your emotional state and draw from your response how they are to respond. It is much like the way we pass on to our children our fear of spiders, snakes, or thunderstorms. They see us afraid and they naturally assume that if the adults in their life are afraid of these things, they too should be afraid.

Presenting the concepts of death and dying to the children in your life in your most mature, loving, honest, and balanced way will help them face and cope with the losses in their life even before they occur. Your modeling of how to address the mystery of death with dignity, courage, caring, and emotional honesty will be your gift to them for the rest of their lives as they follow your example of healthy, sincere grieving.

In talking with children, keep things as concrete as possible, especially with young children. Expect younger children to ask questions about anything and everything — usually at the least opportune and most embarrassing times. Answer their questions directly. If, for example, they ask, "What is that funny smell when we go to visit Grandma?" don't try to come up with something exotic to explain it away. Just tell them straight up what is happening. It is (*a*) the medicine Grandma is taking, (*b*) the disinfectant used to keep Grandma's room clean, (*c*) Grandma's disease, which has made it so she can't control when she goes to the bathroom, etc. You get the idea. Tell the truth. Be patient with them. After all, they are children.

Older children should be given the opportunity to talk about their feelings when they are ready to, but they should not be forced to talk about things if they are not ready. This is especially so with boys, who generally don't talk as much as girls about what is bothering them. I remember one mother who brought her teenage son in to see me several months after his father had passed away. She was convinced that Tommy was suffering from some terrible complication of his grief because he had never shared it with her. As I got to know Tommy, I discovered that he was grieving appropriately for his age, that he did have adults and friends with whom to share his feelings, and that he was generally doing just fine. The real issue, as is often the case, was that Mom was upset because Tommy had not included her in his circle of confidantes.

Like younger children, older children will also follow your example. If you are up tight, judgmental, and closed off, they will not share with you what is going on with them. Share what you are feeling, but be careful you don't lean too heavily on them for emotional support for yourself. If you present yourself as too needy, you may frighten them, and they will be reluctant to share their sorrow with you for fear it will be too much for you to handle. Instead of confiding in you, they may end up feeling emotionally responsible for and protective of you. If, however, you are calm, honest, accepting, open, and adult in what you share, they will know that it is safe to let you know what they feel. Let them know that even though you are hurting too, you care and you are available to talk when they want to talk. But don't crowd them. The teenage years are an emotional roller coaster already. The necessity of facing the death of a close family member adds yet another layer of complication on what is already a confusing time in their lives. Express your thoughts and honest feelings to them. Let them hear you talk about your struggles in dealing with your loss and what you are doing to cope as best you can. Let them know that you don't expect them to have to go through this all alone. Be courageous enough to share that you don't have all the answers, but that you are eager to walk with them as they — and you — face the questions.

One way children of all ages can learn about death and dying is to let them help in caregiving as they are able in age-appropriate ways. School-age children can help to keep water glasses full, bring in newspapers or books, or read to a bed-bound family member. Younger children often enjoy spending time with a dying family member doing quiet crafts, coloring, putting together puzzles, playing games, or just watching TV. Older children can assist with personal care and might even accompany sick family members on medical appointments. Helping out in little ways like this gives children a way to deal with the sense of helplessness we all feel when facing death and will help them to maintain warm relationships with and to create lasting, happy memories of their dying family member.

Another thing you can do for your children at a time of death and dying is to let the significant adults in your children's lives know what your family is going though. Teachers, pastors, Sunday school teachers, Scout or 4-H leaders, dance or piano instructors, coaches, and even the parents of friends whose houses they spend a lot of time at are all your allies and helpers in assisting your children through this difficult time. Being fore-warned, they will be better equipped to interpret the sometimes confusing way children have of expressing unpleasant emotions. Children have a way of acting out their worries in surprising and sometimes inappropriate ways. Younger grade school children have been known to have toileting "accidents" when going through emotionally difficult times. They may revert to thumb sucking or other infantile behaviors they had long ago given up. Children of all ages may become uncharacteristically clingy, aggressive, emotional, or withdrawn, sometimes all at the same time. The quality of their schoolwork may go down. They may want to spend more time at home where they can monitor what is going on. They may look for excuses to stay away from home so they can avoid having to deal with things. Rest assured that these are all normal ways for children to handle grief and that the best thing you can do is to continue to love them unconditionally and include them through it all.

There are many good books on the market that can be of great help in explaining death and dying to children. Some are designed to help parents talk to their children. Others are written for a parent and child to read together. Some are aimed at younger children; others are more appropriate for older children and teenagers. Talk to your clergyperson, a school counselor, or a children's librarian about what they might suggest or ask a clerk at your local bookstore what they would recommend.

Grief Is Powerful

I still remember his face. He was a big man. I am over six feet tall and he loomed over me. I could tell from his build and the way he carried himself that he had once been quite an athlete. When I met him he was probably in his seventies and had long since retired from the U.S. Army, where he had served as a Ranger during the Second World War. He told me that he had seen fighting all over the European front from Scandinavia south to Italy. He told me stories of how he had held friends in his arms as the life oozed out of their shattered bodies, gotten up, and gone back into battle. But here he was now in my office with a look on his face that was somewhere between panic and rage. I could tell he had been crying, but I knew that to mention it would be a great embarrassment to him. He was there because he wanted to know — actually *demanded* to know — how he could have gone through all that he had gone through as a young man and have none of it bother him, only to be totally devastated by the death of his wife a few months before. This big, handsome, brave, strong man had been brought to his knees by this little thing we call "grief."

Emotions are powerful. Often they come in clusters of reinforcing or even conflicting feelings. Take being in love. At any given moment on any given day our feeling toward the object of our love may be longing, tenderness, outrage, lust, disappointment, desire, and/or fear. Still, we lump all these individual feelings together and call it "love." But grief, of all the jumbles of conflicting and changing emotions and thoughts we go through, is perhaps the most powerful emotional cluster of all. As with all emotions, we have only limited intellectual control over grief. So, since we can't think or reason our way out of grief, we are often left believing that grief is uncontrollable, that all we can do is grit our teeth and wait it out, hoping against hope that we don't embarrass ourselves by "breaking down" somewhere or sometime. We cling to the old saying "time heals all wounds" and hope to God it is true.

But if "time heals all wounds," it is equally true that "time wounds all heals." Time certainly dulls the ache of grief, but it does not take it away. To make matters worse, time can complicate grief by hiding it under a false veneer of "just fine." Contrary to popular myth, being passive in the face of grief or trying to ignore it does not make it go any easier. Time in and of itself is no magical cure for grief. But time *along with* thoughtful, intentional interventions can bring relief to the suffering of grief. We do not find relief for our grief by sitting around waiting for the pain and suffering to go away any more than we get back on our feet after we break a leg by sitting on the couch for six months. Returning to our normal, healthy life after a broken leg requires the hard work of physical therapy — what we call rehabilitation. Getting through grief requires a rehabilitation of its own. And it is work, hard work. Grief work is perhaps the hardest work most of us will ever have to do.

Grief Is Sometimes Anticipated

People sometimes wonder why they are starting to feel a sense of loss before the loss has even occurred. Parents, for example, often report a sense of sadness as their last child gets ready to leave home and they anticipate how empty and quiet the house will be without the sounds of children they have known for so many years. What they are experiencing is called "anticipatory grief." Just thinking about or anticipating a loss can trigger feelings of grief. This is what the famous researcher Elisabeth Kübler-Ross discovered in her groundbreaking research on death and dying. Kübler-Ross described how people who were dying would first greet the news with a sense of denial and then move though predictable stages of anger, bargaining, depression, and finally acceptance. We now know that not only do the dying go through these stages; so do those who will be left behind. Grief doesn't start when the loss occurs. It starts when we begin to think of the hopes and dreams we will never see fulfilled. It starts when we begin to envision a life without our loved one present.

Anticipatory grief is often much more powerful than we imagine. One of my friends who read an early draft of this book said that at one point she started crying because just thinking about losing someone close to her filled her with a sense of sadness. I often hear stories of people who find the very thought of loss can send them on a wild emotional spiral. If you are one of these people, I encourage you to reflect on just what it is about loss, death, and dying that you find so upsetting. You may want to write in a journal about your thoughts and feelings about death or talk to trusted friends about how they handle loss. Simply having thought about loss and learning how others have come to incorporate it into their lives will help you to be better prepared to handle loss in a more mature, healing way when it actually occurs in your life.

Grief Involves a Choice

I have good news and I have bad news. The bad news is that grief cannot be avoided. All of God's children will experience loss. We will all grieve. The good news is that we have a choice in how we will approach our experience of grief. We can be a passive victim of grief or an active participant with grief.

Though grief cannot be avoided, we do have a choice of how we will tackle our grief work. We can, if we wish, choose to deny or delay the work of grief by trying to wall off our sense of loss. But trying to deny grief is like trying to deny the steam inside a boiling pot. As the water inside the pot begins to boil, nothing seems to be happening at first. But gradually, as the steam slowly builds up, the pressure starts to lift the lid. At first all we see is just a faint wisp of steam. Then we hear the lid jiggling as more steam demands to get out. We might at this point try to keep the steam trapped inside. We press down on the lid and the jiggling stops. But steam pressure will not be defeated that easily. Before we know it the pressure builds and builds and soon it takes all our attention and strength to keep the lid from blowing off.

Grief acts in much the same way. We can try to keep our grief sealed away, to deny our sense of loss. And we might even be successful for a while. But grief demands to be let out. Just as with the steam in the boiling pot, we can try to keep grief contained, but grief is stronger than we think. The more we refuse to face our sense of loss or the more we push to try to contain it, the more powerful our grief will become until eventually it breaks out and we have to deal with it. Sooner or later the boiling pot of our unresolved sense of loss starts rattling so much that it takes all our energy and attention. This is what happened to the Army Ranger I described above. He had never talked about his experiences of the war, but instead had kept all that grief and loss bottled up for almost fifty years. The death of his wife was that little extra bit of steam that finally blew the lid off and forced him to address his grief for the first time.

Grief Is Unpredictable

Just how grief controls us varies from person to person. You may find yourself drowning in a sea of uncontrollable thoughts and emotions. You may find it hard to concentrate or see yourself doing silly things you would never ordinarily do. One very self-sufficient woman told me she had never locked her keys in her car until after her husband had died. Another woman told me how after her husband died her upper thighs had become a mass of bruises after she had started running into the desks at the office where she had worked for years, although she had never run into them before his death. You might find yourself crying at awkward times. I remember sitting in one of my favorite Mexican restaurants the day after I had to put my old dog to sleep and startling the waitress who had come back to ask if everything was all right. She thought the tears streaming down my face had something to do with the food!

Feelings of loss may dominate your emotional life. You may be troubled with various physical complaints. (*Warning:* It is fairly common for caregivers to start to experience the symptoms of their loved one's illness!)

You might want to sleep all the time, or you might walk the floor night after night unable to get any sleep at all. You may try to stuff your life with activities, projects, or causes only to find that what you hoped would be fulfilling and meaningful only leaves you tired and strangely unsatisfied instead. I actually had to tell a volunteer to go home and not come back when she started showing up at the church every day to do this or that or the other thing about two months after I had buried her husband. She was hurting, and she didn't want to hurt. She thought that if she could just keep herself busy enough doing something worthwhile her hurt would go away.

You might "blow up" or "break down" on people for no apparent reason. Old, comfortable relationships may begin to erode or suffer. You may find yourself pouring out your heart to total strangers. You may have no interest in sex or you may be hornier than ever.

Your religious practice may begin to feel rote and boring, and God may seem more distant than in the past. Or you might find a new depth to your spirituality, and God may never have seemed more real and present to you. You might find yourself in a serious and sober search for spiritual meaning. You might find yourself pursuing the most frivolous and hedonistic, self-serving activity you can think of. Witness all those cruise ships full of "merry widows" looking for love in all the wrong places.

The death, or the pending death, and the unwanted changes it brings may continue to seem meaningless and harsh. You may find yourself emotionally empty or "stuck." One particular concern, especially for those who have addictive tendencies or who come from families where substances have been abused, is that you may find yourself tempted to "medicate" your sadness away. As all those country-and-western songs retell, many is the person who has tried to drown his or her sorrow in caffeine, alcohol, sleeping pills, "pep" pills, or street drugs, only to find they are making things worse for themselves. Yes, grief can be awful, but there is no need to complicate your life even more by going on a "bender" in a futile attempt to make something go away that is not going to go away.

These complications of grief can happen before the loss even occurs. They may show up shortly after the loss, or months or even years later. I personally think that much of the family conflict of "dysfunctional" families may actually be unrecognized and unresolved grief controlling one or more family members. I remember how I prided myself on how well I handled my father's death. After all, I was the trained professional. I knew how to handle these things! But about a year after Dad died I realized that I had been crabby and generally obnoxious for a couple of weeks. When I asked my wife if she had noticed it, she assured me that she had! She also reminded me that it was the anniversary of Dad's death.

"That's it!" I thought to myself. "Of course I'm feeling a little down. I'm glad that's over; now I can go on with my life." Little did I know then that the same vague sensations of loss and dis-ease would occur about the same time of year for the next several years as my body and spirit continued to remember their grief even if my intellect continued to pretend that everything was "just fine."

Make no mistake about it: grief is real, authentic, 100 percent genuine suffering. You can try to deny it, but it won't go away. People might try to talk you out of it, but that won't work either. They may try to make you feel guilty or ashamed for being sad or crying. You might think that you are the exception to the rule: that you will be the one person in history whom grief will leave untouched. But grief is nothing to be ashamed of. It is not something we can avoid. Grief is a universal human experience that touches each and every life.

A Final Word on Grief

"Blessed are those who grieve," said Jesus in the Sermon on the Mount (Matthew 5), "for they will be comforted." Or, in the words of the African American spiritual, "I'm so glad troubles don't last always." The only good thing about grief is that with smart, intentional, hard work and time it does lessen. As "Annie" reminds us, the sun *will* come up tomorrow, be it an earthly sun or a new day in the land beyond the grave. Grief happens. And when grief happens we all, the dying and those left behind, are changed by the experience, often for the better.

I encourage you, then, not to be afraid of grief. Grief is messy. It is not something you can neatly tie up with fancy papers and bows and put away. Rather, grief tends to have a mind of its own. Just when you thought you were done with it, grief is likely to come bouncing out of the closet where you thought you had it all safely tucked away. Your experience of loss will lead you through emotional and spiritual suffering. It is going to touch and change everything about your world. Grief is going to cause you to uncover parts of yourself and your relationships that you never knew existed. But in the end, if you have the courage, the stamina, and the faith to face your loss and handle your grief with care, you will get through it a stronger, wiser, more compassionate and perhaps better person.

I guarantee it.

Chapter Five

How Do I Do This?

Issues Raised in Chapter Four

If you've made it this far through this book, you have proved you are committed to making your experience of death and dying as healing as possible. Now what? So far we've been talking about theory and intentions. Now it is time to get down to the actual work. Below you will find a series of questions based on the issues raised in chapter 4. Working through these questions on your own as well as with your team of caregivers and your care receiver will help you clarify your thinking about them.

Please, do not limit yourself to my questions. I tried my best to cover all the bases, but I'm sure I didn't think of everything. Your situation may have extenuating circumstances that I would never think of and that make careful planning even more important. Get yourself a notebook where you can write out your responses to the questions and jot down additional questions as they come to you.

Issues Concerning Loss

I have suggested that previous experiences of loss can help you find strength on which you can draw to face this moment of death. Take a moment to consider what you have learned over the years.

- Which of these experiences of loss have you had in your life?

    – Moving to new home or city

    – Death of pet(s)

    – Changing schools

    – Friend or relative moving away

    – Empty nest

    – Divorce (your own or that of someone close to you)

    – Loss of personal items through fire, robbery, etc.

    – Death of a close relative

    – Breakup with boyfriend or girlfriend

    – Other

- What made these losses significant to you?
- How did you handle them?
- Where did you find comfort and support?
- Who was helpful to you at that time?
- What did they do or say that was helpful?
- What did you learn about yourself from these experiences?
- What did you learn about loss, death, and dying from these experiences?
- What would you have done differently?
- What do you wish others would have said or done differently?
- What strength did you find in yourself that you can draw on now?

Issues Concerning Grief

Grief comes in many styles. Understanding your own grieving patterns can prepare you to bear grief more intentionally. Sharing your insights into your personal grieving patterns with others can help to create an atmosphere of trust where different ways of grieving are accepted.

- What scares you the most as you anticipate dealing with death and dying?

- Do you tend to grieve more privately and internally, or do you grieve more openly and externally?

- How will others know you are actively grieving?

- What do you anticipate you may need from the others to make it through the coming weeks and months?

- What can you offer to the others as they face their grief?

- What would you like others to do if you start to cry?

Helping Children

No one likes to think of having to prepare children to lose a loved one. Consider here some of the ways you can help the young people in your life to face the reality of death and dying with grace and courage.

- What were you told about death and dying when you were young?

- What was helpful about what you were told?

- What was not helpful?

- What are the names and ages of the children in your family? What developmental stages are they in? (Consulting with a teacher or school counselor can help you identify developmental stages.)

- What experiences of death or loss have they had?

  - Major move

  - Death of a pet

  - Loss of a neighbor

  - Major news story that caught their attention

  - Loss of significant a possession

  - Divorce in the family

  - Friend moving away

- Change of school building or system
- Death of a distant relative
- Death of a close relative
- Experience of theft or robbery
- Other

• How can you draw from those experiences to help them now?

• How can you keep the children connected to what your family is going through?

• What tasks could they help with?

• Who are the significant adults in your children's lives and who will contact them?

- Aunts, uncles, grandparents, older siblings
- Teachers, child care providers
- Coaches, private teachers, tutors
- Scout leaders, 4-H Club leaders
- Pastor, Sunday school teacher, youth leader
- Best friends' parents
- Employers
- Other significant adults

• What books, movies, or CDs do you have to help explain death and dying to the children?

• Where could you get additional resources?

• What words and images will you use to describe what is going on?

• What complications or special needs do you anticipate in talking to the children about death and dying?

Chapter Six

Healing When a Cure
Is No Longer Possible

It would be nice to be able to say that medical science had found a cure for every hurt and pain. It would be nice to be able to say that every trip to the doctor's office or hospital resulted in complete recovery. It would be nice to be able to say that doctors were able to put us back together again no matter what silly thing we did to hurt ourselves. But the reality is that there are many illnesses and injuries no physician or surgeon can successfully treat. The reality is that death happens. And when it does, grief is unavoidable.

Sometimes death and grief come suddenly, as in a traffic accident. More often than not though, barring accidents, we have some kind of warning that death is coming. Advances in medical science have combined to keep us alive much longer now so that, instead of dying from acute infections or massive bleeding from cutting ourselves on a plow while digging up the back forty or from childbirth, most people in North America today die from cancer, heart disease, emphysema, HIV/AIDS, or some other chronic condition. More often than not we live with weeks or months or even years of knowing of the condition that will one day take our life.

And so we are faced with an interesting dilemma our ancestors seldom had to face: how do we live, knowing that death is near, without letting the knowledge of the nearness of death rob us of the life we have left? Or, to put it another way: how can we allow our experience of dying to enrich and complete our experience of living, however long life lasts?

All too often the answer to the question of how to live with the knowledge of impending death is either to deny that the fatal condition is real and pretend it doesn't exist or to fall into despair and abandon all hope for a meaningful existence no matter how long or short it may be.

Some people simply refuse to allow themselves to think about death. They greet the news of a life-threatening diagnosis with either a blank stare or angry rejection. Only recently I visited a church member who was in the hospital diagnosed with two unrelated conditions. The first, a severe but easily curable problem, he talked about quite readily in an almost embarrassed tone of voice, as if he were self-conscious about being sick at all. The other condition, a chronic, much more serious and potentially life-threatening one, he didn't mention. In fact, if his wife had not been there I wouldn't have found out about it at all. When she mentioned it to me he gave a dismissive snort and rolled over in bed, turning his back to me. The message was clear: as far as he was concerned, he was *not* going to have this condition no matter what the doctors, his wife, or I had to say about it!

Other people dwell on their terminal diagnosis, allowing it to put them in their grave long before they have left the earth. As one nurse I used to work with put it, they "fold their tent" and prepare to move on even though they may have weeks, months, or years of life left to them. They lose interest in friends, family, and favorite pursuits. They become depressed and may even become incommunicative. They wall themselves off in an attempt to spare themselves any more pain or suffering.

What is common to both these reactions to the news of fatal illness is that they are both basically dishonest. To either deny death in the face of continuing life or deny life in the face of coming death is to play games with the truth. It is a cowardly way to attempt to avoid the suffering of grief that accompanies the news of death and dying. It is to play games with ourselves and the ones who love us.

And I need to mention that these strategies are often attempted not only by the dying, but by loved ones as well. I am reminded of the woman who continued to fix full-course meals for her dying husband long after he had lost the ability to chew and swallow solid food. Every mealtime became a scene of heartbreak and frustration as she tried and tried to get him to eat and he was simply unable to do so. After the meal he would lie in the bed exhausted from the attempt to satisfy her wishes, feeling terrible about disappointing her again. Meanwhile she tearfully carried the barely touched tray of food back to the kitchen, silently accusing herself for her inability to fix something he would actually eat. Likewise we probably all have heard of friends and loved ones who simply stop calling or visiting once they hear word of a terminal illness. They often use excuses like "I can't stand the smell of disinfectant," or "I don't like hospitals." Anything to avoid admitting what is really going on: they are just plain afraid of the specter of death.

Still, as harsh as I may sound, I can't blame people for trying either of these defensive strategies. Having gone through the grief of the loss of my father, I know what they are trying to avoid. But I also know that neither denial nor despair is the answer. Neither denial nor despair will keep death at bay, and neither will reduce the suffering of the individual who is dying or that of family and friends.

It doesn't have to be this way. We cannot avoid death or dying or the grief that follows. We can, though, with courage, honesty, and faith meet the work of death, dying, and grief head-on. Even when a cure for our bodies is not possible, healing for our minds and souls is always possible.

When the reality of death, dying, and grief happens we have a choice to make: to be a passive victim *of* grief, or to be an active participant *with* grief. If you had decided to be a passive victim, you would have put this book down a long time ago. Since you are still reading, I am going to assume that you have decided to be an active participant.

What Works for You

Before we get to the strategies, there is one last thing we need to discuss. One of the things that complicates this custom-fit experience of death and dying I am encouraging you to develop is worrying about what others think. Everybody these days seems to have an opinion on how you are supposed to handle death and dying. Some advocate a form of denial by suggesting that the less you think about it the better off you will be. Others encourage you to go quietly, not to fight it, but to allow "nature to take its course." Some tell you that you have to take certain steps in a certain order to make things come out right in the end.

Bless their hearts! They think they are looking out for your best interests, but all they really know is what works for them. Their style may or may not work for you. Only *you* know what you need right here and right now to get through this time. If you or someone you love is dying, *don't worry about what someone else thinks* about you or someone else's emotional state or how it is expressed. Don't worry about whether or not they think you are "doing it right." There are no mistakes in coping with death and dying. There is only what works for you as you. If you are being sincere, truthful, and faithful in seeking wholeness and healing for yourself and those around you, you are doing just fine.

Once again, remember, no matter what anyone tells you, you cannot control your experience of death, dying, and grief. You can only manage it in a way that brings healing and wholeness to you and those you love. Death, dying, and grief are out of our control, but we can be in charge of how we are going to experience what we are going through.

Creating a Healing Experience of Death

I know I've already said it, but I'm going to keep on saying it because it bears saying again: there is no way to control the emotional tornado we call grief. Grief picks you up off your feet and takes you to places you don't want to go. It is painful, frustrating, scary, and exhausting. However, we are not totally helpless in the face of loss and grief.

I grew up in Ohio. Tornadoes occur in Ohio, but are relatively rare compared to other areas of the country. Hurricanes are even rarer, happening only once every few years when one travels up from the Gulf Coast and even then, when they arrive, they are in a much weakened state. I've always wondered how people can stand to live in Kansas or Oklahoma, where it seems summer is just full of twisters. Or what would it be like to live in Florida, where hurricanes — sometimes more than one — happen every year? I freak out at the thought of a tornado bearing down on me. The thought of actually living through a hurricane is beyond my imagination. And all I'm talking about so far is just a little wind. How do people possibly live in areas where there are major earthquakes, forest fires, or overwhelming floods?

I am, obviously, a bit of a natural disaster wimp. But for people who live where tornadoes, hurricanes, earthquakes, forest fires, and floods are likely to occur, they are just a part of life. They learn how to take them in stride. They learn to look for warning signs and to take emergency announcements seriously. They keep emergency food and water around the house. They stock up on batteries for flashlights and radios. They build storm shelters under their houses, add storm shutters to their windows, or make other modifications to their homes to make them more disaster resistant. They keep fire extinguishers ready and may have a generator to provide electricity in case of a long power outage. They may even have an escape route planned and know just where they can go if they have to evacuate.

But, even though I'm from Ohio, I am not totally helpless in the face of Mother Nature's fury. I lived in the snow belt area along Lake Erie for almost twenty years. I may not know how to handle a hurricane or a massive forest fire, but I do know how to handle a snowstorm very well. I keep a windshield scraper in my car and a snow shovel in my garage. I keep the antifreeze and window washer fluids filled in the car. I know to keep the gas tank in my car from getting too low. I know how to steer out of a skid on the highway. I drive on all-weather tires. I know to keep faucets slightly open so the pipes won't freeze if the power goes out. I know the importance of insulation, weather stripping, and storm windows. I own several warm coats, hats, gloves, long johns, and boots and know how to dress in layers to keep warm when it gets cold. I might be a basket case in Florida in hurricane season, but my Florida relatives would be positively awed by the way I know how to handle snow and cold. Why, I am so courageous in face of snow and cold that I actually go outside *on purpose* to ski and sled in what to them is something terrible to endure.

What I am getting at is simply this: equipping ourselves with the tools and knowledge we need to handle the "normal" natural disasters that are likely in our part of the world gives us the confidence we need to handle safely and comfortably what nature throws at us. In the same way we can prepare ourselves with the tools and knowledge we need to handle grief with relative calm and confidence, growing through the process into a healthier, more whole — maybe even more holy? — person.

There is no one simple, all-purpose recipe for putting together a healing experience of death, just as there is not one way of preparing for a tornado, hurricane, or snowstorm. The spiritual and psychological demands brought on by loss are not nearly as controllable as we modern, scientifically minded people would like them to be. However, we need not wait till the moment death arrives to begin our work of grief. My experience, and that of hundreds of others, is that those who move *toward* their anticipated loss rather than *away* from it find they can reduce the suffering involved in death and dying. Also, they learn that their grief, though painful, is less devastating than that of those who try to deny what is happening to them.

There are ways we can actively create an atmosphere for ourselves and those around us in which a healing experience of death is more likely to occur. Just as in all ventures of the heart, there are no guarantees that things will go as you expect. It will take wisdom, courage, and stamina. You will have good days and bad days. You will probably wonder more than once if the effort is worth it. You may even curse the day you picked up this book and held out for yourself the hope that your grief might lessened. Still, I invite you to take a chance on yourself and those you love. I offer you the following eight areas of concern and strategies for handling them as the colors you will need to cover the blank canvas of your movement through death, dying, and grief.

Who Does What?

Ideally these strategies would be put into practice by a family or community of friends who, together with the person who is dying, would covenant to come together to find healing when a cure is no longer possible. I realize that this ideal is not always going to be realized. Not only does our consumer-driven, pleasure-first culture encourage us to avoid delving into the places death and dying takes us, but, to be honest about it, life gets complicated. Many of us have schedules and responsibilities that make it difficult to simply drop everything and devote ourselves to caring for someone who is dying, no matter how much we might want to. Many of us have jobs that have taken us away from home, and we now find that distance alone is an all but insurmountable barrier to caring for a dying family member. Also, family spats and long standing feuds can make it difficult to come together at this emotionally trying time.

So it should come as no surprise if one or more of your family or the group of friends you were counting on to help with this work is just not interested or able to participate. We also have to be honest in admitting that some of us have been so damaged by family dysfunction, addiction, abuse, or life experiences that we can only participate in this kind of activity in a limited way, if at all. I will talk about some of these extenuating circumstances and what you can do to handle them later on. For now, though, I encourage you to read on. You don't have to wait until you have the ideal situation to create a healing experience of death. If only a few of those involved, or only you alone, attempt to honestly and intentionally attend to these eight items you will be preparing your heart and mind for the peace you seek. And, much to everyone's surprise, you will also influence the others who cannot or will not participate.

Strategies for Healing

The eight strategies for finding healing when a cure is no longer possible are as follows:

1. Paying Attention to the Details of Dying

For the experience of death to be healing, the individuals involved —
especially the person who is dying — must have a sense that they have as
much to say as possible about the decisions that affect care and comfort.
Though some may find this self-evident, it comes as shocking news to
others: in the face of death and dying it is *people*, not symptoms, policies,
schedules, professional reputations, family expectations, egos, or lines of
authority that come first. And the number *one* person who needs to be in
the driver's seat is the person with the terminal illness.

So if your experience of death is to be healing, you — all of you — are
going to have to talk about it. Now, that's hard. I know it is. None of us
likes to think about our own demise. None of us likes to hear someone we
love talk about what is going to happen when they aren't around anymore.
It is tempting to want to sit back and let someone else be in charge, to
let someone else make the hard decisions that have to be made. Still, as
painful and difficult as it is, it is vital that you all talk about these things
as early in the dying process as possible.

I have witnessed over and over that the person who is dying and his or
her caregivers each do want to talk about these things, but they hesitate
to bring them up for fear of upsetting the other. I can't tell you how many
times the dying person or a family member has drawn me aside to talk
about the terminal condition, begging me to say nothing to other family
members.

Over and over I've had to encourage them to stop using me as a sound-
ing post and talk to each other instead. Will your loved one be upset if
you tell them you know they are dying? Perhaps they will be, but my experience tells me that they will be relieved that you know and now you
can both talk about it together. If you have not already done this, I encourage you to dare to take the risk to be open. If things are not talked
out early on, the uncertainty of how to proceed can create untold conflict
and heartache later on when family members and friends, caught up in
the suffering of their grief, end up having emotional disagreements about
what to do and when to do it.

I encourage you to talk together about the many details of death and dying as soon after the terminal diagnosis as possible, while everyone is still relatively fresh, emotionally and physically. This increases the likelihood of the dying person's wishes being met and decreases the chance that survivors will end up second guessing themselves or squabbling over minor issues later on. Focus on the person and not the situation. With a lot of patience, love, and grace — and a big box of tissues — you *can* get through these difficult heart-to-heart talks and together come up with a plan that everyone can live, and die, with.

There are several components to taking charge of the dying process, but probably the best place to start is to get the wishes of the dying person down on paper. There are four legal tools that can help you with this. They are (1) a *Living Will*, (2) a *Durable Power of Attorney for Health Care*, (3) a *Durable Power of Attorney*, and (4) a *Last Will and Testament*.

Though details may vary from state to state, a *Living Will* spells out what kind of or the degree to which "heroic measures" will be performed by medical personnel in the case of a life-threatening emergency situation. Often people think about a Living Will in terms of whether or not to "pull the plug." But there is a lot more to it than that. Depending on the illness or injury, you may be presented with a whole list of procedures that the person who is dying may or may not wish to have performed as the end of life nears. The options include:

Intubation a breathing tube is inserted into the windpipe and attached to a machine that will force air into the lungs when the person is too weak to breathe unassisted.

Heart defibrillation electrical paddles are used to shock the heart into regular rhythm.

Artificial hydration and/or nourishment a naso-gastric (NG) tube is run through the nose into the stomach, or is surgically inserted directly into the stomach (a "peg" tube); through it food and water can be pumped.

Medications everything from medicines designed to treat the disease (e.g., chemotherapy) to a whole range of pain medicines is to be considered.

This list is not meant to be exhaustive. Depending on the conditions — whether you are doing care at home or are using a healthcare facility, the level of insurance coverage, the competence and willingness of home care-givers to learn how to use various devices and to administer medications, and a host of other variables — you may have more or fewer options to consider. Sometimes these measures are used to keep a severely ill person comfortable. Sometimes they are used to prolong dying beyond what is appropriate. The question you have to answer is this: what does the person who is dying want done, for how long, and when is enough enough? A Living Will is your chance to record all this and make sure that everyone is literally on the same page.

There are two more things you need to know about Living Wills. First, it is not uncommon for family members or friends to panic when they see their loved one's health take a sudden and dramatic decline. If they are not prepared to see the person they love begin to have labored breathing, experience a dramatic drop in energy, or show some other symptom of nearing death, they may forget all about the Living Will and call emergency services. Once EMS have been called, they are required *by law* to do everything they can to preserve life regardless of what the Living Will says. So, make sure *everyone* who is likely to be around when the moment of death comes knows the contents of the Living Will, particularly if the person who is dying has opted to die at home. Some people actually go so far as to put a big "Do not call 911 (EMS)" sign on each phone in the house.

The other thing you need to know about Living Wills is that they are written on paper, not in stone. You are allowed to change your mind. The person who is dying might tell everyone he doesn't want any heroic measures taken, and then decide he does. She might have given instructions for all or certain measures to be taken and then later decide she is tired and wants things to come to an end. Remember, the dying person is in the driver's seat. Let her or him take charge!

The second tool to help you take charge of the dying process is the *Durable Power of Attorney for Health Care*. This legal document names one particular person as the official spokesperson if decisions about care arise and the person who is dying is no longer able to communicate. This is different from a regular Power of Attorney, which you might sign when you buy a house, giving an employee of the lending institution permission to agree to certain minor details of the deal on your behalf in your absence. A regular Power of Attorney ends when the specific act you authorized to be performed on your behalf is completed. It is not "durable." A Durable Power of Attorney for Health Care gives the designated spokesperson the authority to speak on behalf of the dying person for as long as necessary in regard to health care needs.

To be someone's voice when he or she can no longer speak for himself or herself is an awesome responsibility. Also, it is hard to imagine asking someone to take on such a burden. Still, it is very important that you do, as it gives family and friends as well as the medical team someone to turn to when a decision is needed at a critical moment and emotions may be running high. I have seen horrible, protracted, painful family disputes arise at the moment of death when there have been major disagreements over what to do and no one had been designated as the "official" voice.

So encourage the dying person to give careful thought about who will be asked to do this. Be honored if your loved one asks you to serve in this way. Be sure that the two of them (or the two of you) take time to talk so that both are clear about what should or should not happen. And don't talk about it just once. Keep in conversation with one another so that as changes in physical status come and go any changes in wishes can be honored.

A third document you might consider is a simple *Durable Power of Attorney*. This document allows someone to make financial decisions, to sign checks, and to have access to bank accounts. This is particularly helpful in case there is not a spouse who would normally assume this function or when a spouse in unable to take on this responsibility due to age or illness. Often the Durable Power of Attorney for Health Care and the Durable Power of Attorney for financial decisions are given to the same person, say a son or a daughter. Sometimes the Durable Power of Attorney for financial decisions is given to a trusted banker or lawyer (who may charge for this service) while a close friend or family member is named to make medical decisions. What is most important is that someone is named and that everyone who is likely to be involved with the care team knows who this person is.

Finally, the fourth document everybody needs to have is a simple *Last Will and Testament*. A will is a way to say what is to be done with one's possessions — one's estate — when a person dies. Without a will, the state in which you live will make those decisions, taking a healthy slice of the assets on the way. A will can also state who you would want your minor children to stay with if you should die while they are still young. When putting together a will, you will be asked to name an "executor," the person who will be legally responsible to see that the provisions of your will are carried out according to your wishes. An executor can be anyone you want: a friend, a child, a spouse, or even your attorney. You might want to give all your Durable Powers of Attorney to the person who will eventually be your executor. You might want to divide these tasks.

If you have questions about a Living Will, speak to your physician or attorney. An intake nurse or social worker at the hospital can also be of help. If you have questions about what your faith tradition allows regarding end-of-life decisions, contact a clergyperson of your faith tradition or ask to speak to a hospital chaplain. An attorney can help you with all the other documents.

Though I am presenting these documents as tools to help you at the end of life, you don't have to wait until you have a terminal illness to have them drawn up. As the poet reminds us, "tomorrow is promised to no one." It is a good idea to make your wishes regarding end-of-life decisions known to those who are close to you even though you are in prime health. Again, I can't count the number of times I've sat with a family as death draws near and no one has a clue about what the dying person's wishes are. No one had ever brought it up before. If the idea of getting formal paperwork drawn up creeps you out, *please* at least *talk* with your loved ones about these things while you can do so with some sense of calm detachment. Even if it's just a casual conversation in the back yard after a picnic dinner, you owe it to yourself and those you love to give them *some* idea of what you would like to have done. Then, if something sudden and unexpected happens, they will at least know your intentions even if they are not written down.

One stumbling block to getting all this work done is finding an attorney who can help without charging an exorbitant fee to do it. If you don't have an attorney of your own, ask around among family and friends. If they can't give you any good leads, you can contact your local bar association for a list of family law attorneys in your area.

In addition to legal and medical decisions, you will also want to get your financial house in order. Those who have ample financial means will probably already have a financial advisor, accountant, or attorney who can help them develop the proper financial documents to protect their resources and see to the care of survivors. Trusts, insurance policies, annuities, savings accounts, certificates of deposit, and other instruments are all to be considered. Those with more modest financial resources will still want to make sure that their money and property are safe and that they go to the persons they intend to receive then. It is possible that the attorney who helps you draw up your will can also help you with your financial paperwork. Another resource is an officer at your local bank.

Yet another aspect of getting your financial house in order is getting all your papers, deeds, records, and account information together. This also includes the addresses, log-on names, and passwords of e-accounts on the Internet. This is especially important in the case of a family where the person who is dying has been the one who had taken care of the family finances. I remember one woman who told me how furious she had been when she came home from work one day and found that her husband, who had been diagnosed with terminal cancer, had taped a sheet of paper inside the kitchen cupboard listing all the bank and insurance account numbers, who to contact, phone numbers, addresses, etc. She didn't want to think about any of that just then and his note only reminded her that their time together was brief. Later, after he was gone, she was enormously grateful that he had been so considerate and forward thinking in putting this information together for her.

One more thing to talk about is funeral or memorial plans, what to do with the body — whether it is to be buried or cremated. One family

I worked with recently got into a heated argument when the husband died suddenly. The wife, who wanted to be cremated, thought that would be a good thing for her husband, too. One of the children, though, was adamant that his father did not want to "be burned up." Try as they might, they couldn't remember ever actually hearing him say what he wanted. Later in this book I will give you some questions to consider as you think together about funeral plans.

One last area that seems trivial compared to the questions we've been addressing is what to do with all the "stuff." Some of it — for example, jewelry and photos — will be kept as treasured family heirlooms. Some of it will find a home with children and friends. Some of it, to be brutally honest about it, is just junk and will need to be given away or thrown out. Often family members would like to have a memento to remember a loved one by. Often these are just trinkets of little monetary value. For years after he died, I kept a mortar and pestle that had been on my father's prescription counter at the drugstore he had owned when I was young. One aunt of mine kept a roll of masking tape and a marker in the living room toward the end of her life. Everyone who visited her was encouraged to "Put your name on something." She wanted no squabbles about what belonged to whom after she was gone.

2. Talking about Religious/Spiritual Issues

We are living in changing religious times. While opinion polls consistently tell us that almost all Americans believe in God in some form or other, these same polls tell us that fewer and fewer people find that the churches, temples, synagogues, or mosques they attended as children still speak to them as they become adults and that there are more people than ever who have grown up with no formal spiritual/religious training at all. Polls also suggest that even as interest in spiritual things increases, attendance at formal worship services remains steady or is decreasing. This suggests that in a society that is increasingly "spiritual," fewer and fewer people practice "organized religion." Still, regardless of what the polls say, there is an almost universal interest in talking about spiritual issues and the possibility of an afterlife as the death of a loved one approaches.

This leads to some interesting and contradictory thoughts and feelings on the part of many people. I have known people who have not been particularly intentional about their spiritual practice who are embarrassed by their sudden interest in spiritual things as they approach death. If you or your loved one feels that way, please don't. It is natural to question the meaning of life as the end of life as we know it approaches. This is a part of the human need to find meaning and to solve problems. Our minds abhor a vacuum and will not abide thinking that "that's all there is." There is nothing hypocritical in a person who has not been involved in religion seeking the comfort and support of a religious or spiritual tradition in the face of death.

If people who do not have much of an intentional spiritual life have questions about spiritual things as death nears, so do people who are active in their spiritual practice. Individuals who already have an active religious or spiritual life often find their relationship with their tradition challenged by the imminence of death.

Some active believers find a new appreciation for the teachings of their religious or spiritual tradition as the end of life draws near. Prayer, scripture reading, and participation in the rites and rituals of their faith tradition may take on a whole new depth of meaning. New forms of prayer might be explored. They may discover a new sense of tolerance and graciousness toward others as they focus on the universals of their religion's teachings rather than on the particular dogmas that tend to keep religious parties at odds. They may feel called to invite others to share their deepened sense of spiritual meaning by initiating gatherings as a family to pray, read the scriptures, sing hymns, or simply share a moment of silence together.

Other people find the anger and confusion they feel about dying or losing a loved one to death makes the normal practice of their religious customs difficult or impossible even if they have been lifelong believers. They might find themselves angry with God. They might want to blame God for causing their heartbreak. And then, as if all this weren't enough, these feelings of anger and resentment toward God may then be followed by feelings of shame or guilt at being angry or resentful toward God. (After all, *real* believers wouldn't feel this way, would they?)

I have known people who have long enjoyed a rich prayer life and who wanted to pray about what was happening to them but found the closeness of death left them unable to put their thoughts and feelings into words. People who found comfort and inspiration from reading the scriptures have found them suddenly meaningless. Church members who have been regulars in their attendance at services have told me they just can't bring themselves to come. Again, this is more common than you might think.

I remember how I, too, had many of these same feelings of anger and resentment at God when I first learned that my dad had cancer. Dad was very involved with his church. I was an ordained pastor who had dedicated my life and career to God's work. Weren't we entitled to a few blessings? How about just a break? I wondered what to do with these angry and uncomfortable spiritual thoughts and feelings. Then I noticed how many of the Psalms are expressions of the same feelings of anger, fear, vengeance, abandonment, and hurt that I was feeling. Thoughts and feelings I was embarrassed to admit to were openly expressed right there in the Bible:

> I am weary with my moaning;
> every night I flood my bed with tears;
> I drench my couch with my weeping.
> My eyes waste away because of grief.
>
> (Ps. 6:6–7)

> Why, O Lord, do you stand far off?
> Why do you hide yourself in times of trouble?
>
> (Ps. 10:1)

> How long, O Lord? Will you forget me forever?
> How long will you hide your face from me?
> How long must I bear pain in my soul
> and have sorrow in my heart all day long?
>
> (Ps. 13:1–2)

My God, my God, why have you forsaken me?
Why are you so far from helping me,
from the words of my groaning? (Ps. 22:1)

Save me, O God,
for the waters have come up to my neck.
I sink in deep mire
where there is no foothold;
I have come into deep waters
and the flood sweeps over me.
I am weary with my crying;
my throat is parched.
My eyes grow dim
with waiting for my God. (Ps. 69:103)

O God, why do you cast us off forever? (Ps. 74:1)

Remember, O Lord, against the Edomites...
Happy shall they be who take [their] little ones
And dash them against the rock! (Ps. 137:7, 9)

Imagine my surprise! Right there in the Bible, in front of God and everyone, was all the frustration and spiritual uncertainty I was feeling! That's when I realized that if I truly believe that God is a God of love and compassion who works all things together for good, why would I need to hide my anger and resentment from God? Not feeling angry or confused when death and grief threaten to turn my world upside down isn't being spiritual. It's being psychotic! God gave us the ability to feel anger, sadness, confusion, resentment, fear, worry, and all those other unpleasant feelings for just this purpose: to express our grief. *Not* to feel and express them at the appropriate time is either to be so far out of touch with reality as to be dangerous to ourselves and others, or to somehow think of ourselves as better than God.

Not to rant and rave at God and the world in the face of such an intolerable situation as death is to be less than honest. How could I say I trusted God if I were to try to keep such an important, life-changing experience as death out of my prayers? How could I claim to have a close relationship with God if I were not willing to share my most deeply held thoughts and feelings — even my anger and disappointment?

I have met a lot of people in my years of work. Most of them are superficial acquaintances, not close personal friends. The difference between an acquaintance and a friend is that I share what is going on in my heart and soul with my friends, while with acquaintances I just exchange polite pleasantries. I let my friends into my inner world and eagerly enter theirs. My friends know my hidden weaknesses as well as my strengths and I know theirs, and we love each other in spite of them. Acquaintances I keep at a comfortable arm's length, close enough to have a relationship of sorts, but never really touching what is truly important. One of the things I learned from my father's death is that if I was going to have a meaningful relationship with God, I was going to have to risk moving beyond being an acquaintance of God and dare to see if I could let God be my friend. I was going to have to let God see all of me, the ugly parts I want to keep hidden as well as the pretty ones I want everyone to know.

I encourage you, then, to acknowledge to yourself *and* to God all of your feelings of anger and confusion as well as your feelings of faithfulness and trust. Express them to trusted friends and family members. Tell them to God. You don't have to know how to pray. Just talk ... or whisper ... or scream. God will hear you. Some people keep a written journal where they can pour out their thoughts and feelings and prayers and then go back over them later and reflect on the progress they've made. Some people like to talk into a tape recorder. Some people paint their prayers, or sing their prayers, or cook their prayers, or garden their prayers, or hike their prayers. It doesn't matter how you do it. What is important is that you find a way to truthfully and humbly open your soul to God, allowing all the beauty and brokenness therein to be trusted to God's loving heart.

Some people find it helpful to talk with a clergyperson, hospital chaplain, pastoral counselor, religious friend, or other identified religious "expert" who is willing to help them wrestle with their questions about death and afterlife. Whoever you select, I encourage you to find someone who will talk with you without demanding that you adopt his or her point of view on these matters. You are already going through a lot. The last thing you need is someone trying to put a spiritual hammerlock on you at this emotionally trying moment.

I was talking with someone just the other day whose brother-in-law was putting pressure on his mother, who was in the final stages of renal failure, to "accept Jesus as her personal savior" before it was too late. As we talked it became clear that his mother had a rich and meaningful relationship with God. She had raised her children in the church and had served God all her life. However, since she had not "come to Jesus" in the way her son-in-law expected, he was convinced that she would not go to heaven. The spiritual problem was not something the mother was feeling; it was the son-in-law's issue. I encouraged him to find a way to speak to his brother-in-law and share with him just how spiritually secure his mother was even if she expressed it differently from what he wanted to hear.

If someone tries to maneuver you into making some kind of spiritual decision, to be "saved" according to how they understand what that means, go very, very slowly. As sincere as they are in offering to you what for them is spiritually meaningful and comforting, decisions made in desperate times and out of strong emotion are seldom good decisions in the long run. Trust that God is already at work in your heart and soul and that you will come to the decision of salvation, hope, and comfort at the time and place that is right for you. That may end up looking like something they wanted, or it may not. What is important is what is going on between you and God.

Most of the religious professionals I know would be happy to talk with you or your loved one about these things no matter what your usual religious practice. I remember years ago getting a call from one of our local hospitals notifying me that a man had asked for me to come and see him. I didn't recognize the name but thought that perhaps he was a former member of the church whose name was no longer on the rolls. When I went to see him, I discovered that he had not practiced any particular religion, but now that he was dying had begun to ask for prayer. We talked for a while and prayed and I promised to stop by and see him again. I did go back and see him, several times, and we began to establish a relationship of trust. It was on one of these subsequent visits that I learned that a Roman Catholic priest and a Jewish rabbi were also seeing him. Here was a man who wasn't taking any chances. He wasn't sure of the answers, but he was taking all the spiritual help he could get!

So, use this time for you and your loved one to explore spiritual and religious instincts. Ask family members and close friends to share their thoughts on life and death. Ask them to pray for and with you. Examine the sacred writings of your faith tradition. If you have not been practicing your faith, consider going to services. Explore a religious bookstore's shelves or prowl the religion section of a secular bookstore. Check out the religion, spirituality, death and dying, and grief sections of your local library for books that speak to your questions. Above all, don't be afraid or ashamed of your spiritual or religious questions. Embrace them. Turn them around and over and upside-down. Give them a good shake. Share your thoughts and questions with others. Pray, even if you don't know how. Take care of your spiritual self. It's an important part of who you are.

3. Reviewing Your Life's Story

One of the things that separates humans from other intelligent beings is that we have the ability to reflect on our lives. Dogs, dolphins, and other higher mammals have the demonstrated ability to remember commands, persons, places, and other things. They can "learn." Higher mammals can even express emotions. But human beings can do more than simply store vast amounts of information and express feelings. Humans have the unique ability to attribute meaning to, draw lessons from, and try to make sense of the things that happen to them. Some researchers even go so far as to say that the human brain is wired in such a way that we not only *can* reflect, attribute, and try to understand, but we *must*.*

It is important for a dying person to have a chance to talk about past pleasures and pains, accomplishments and regrets, successes and failures. It is also important for loved ones to share their memories of these events with the dying person and with each other. Sharing tears and laughter

---

*Andrew Newberg, Eugene D'Aquila, and Vince Rause, *Why God Won't Go Away: Brain Science and the Biology of Belief* (New York: Ballantine, 2001).

over old photos, films, or video can help to create a moment of thankful celebration for the life of the one who is dying and can help those who will survive put those memories into a loving context in which they can be cherished.

The time of death and dying is a great time to collect "oral histories." Take this time to help your loved one tell life stories. Family members, particularly children, love to hear about when their elders were young, especially if they grew up in a different country or in a vastly different context than their own, say a farm, when they know them only as city dwellers. I will cherish forever sitting around the fireplace in my grand-father's basement when I was young listening as he told about his trips to Canada back before there was indoor plumbing or electricity at the fishing camp he and his pals went to year after year. All fish stories are whoppers, and his were great!

Ask those questions you never got around to asking:

1. What were your hopes and dreams when you were young?

2. What was the best job you ever had?

3. Who was your best friend when you were a kid?

4. If you were to do it again, what would you change? What would you keep the same?

5. What do you remember about your parents? Grandparents?

6. What was the most embarrassing moment of your life?

7. Is there anything you regret you never got to do?

8. What books, people, ideas, events most influenced your life? Why? How?

9. What have been the most significant changes you've witnessed over your lifetime?

10. What did you learn about death and dying when you were young?

11. Where was the most interesting place you ever lived?

12. What was the most frightening thing you ever had to go through?

Some people like to write these stories down or record them electronically so they can be kept for future generations to enjoy.

By all means include children in these life reviews. Children love looking at pictures and joining adults in telling "I remember when . . ." stories. Children love to hear how rotten their parents were when they were children. You remember: like the time you put your brother in the dryer, or your sister in a drawer, or tied your siblings' doors shut so they couldn't get out on Christmas morning to open presents. As children hear stories about other people who have come and gone over the years, it helps them to realize that life is full of entrances and exits. It helps them to see that joy and sorrow, beginnings and endings, celebration and grief are all a normal part of the rhythm of life. It is a gentle and safe way for them to begin to experience their loss and for everyone to have a chance to say goodbye.

Let's stop here for a minute. It's time for a reality check. I've been describing this beautiful, idealistic, Norman Rockwell–like scene where families gather to share a smile and a tear and tell their stories of how much they love and care for each other. This is wonderful when it happens, but if we are going to be honest about it, it doesn't always happen quite this way.

Few of us live in perfect families. Many of us harbor memories that are painful, embarrassing, or worse. Many, perhaps most of us, have had some dark chapters in our lives — times when we were victims of our own or someone else's internal demons, times when we compromised our values or beliefs, times when we mistreated or even abused those closest to us, times we made foolish or harmful decisions, times of which we are now not proud. Our families and friends may know all about some or many of these events. Others may have remained hidden away. The time of death and dying offers a time to "come clean." It is a time to ask for, offer, and accept forgiveness for past wrongs. It is a time to confess our sins and accept pardon. It would be my prayer that all those who read these words would go to their grave with a clean conscience and that they could say goodbye to their loved ones knowing that everything that needed to be said was said and the books were clean. It would be my hope that every family member and loved one left behind would be able to visit their loved one's grave knowing that all hurts and resentments were behind them.

But I know that is not going to happen, not for all of us, not for everything. Some of the things that happen over a lifetime are just too hard to talk about, or to listen to. My advice is this: be gentle with yourself and one another. Say what has to be said. Confess your sins to one another, but don't expect to right every wrong you've ever committed or that has ever been committed against you.

The great religions of the world tell us there is a final time of reckoning. They suggest that if something is not addressed in this life, it will be addressed in the next. The reality is that we will all have some questions that will never be answered in this lifetime. Alcoholics Anonymous, perhaps the most spiritually demanding self-help organization in the world, advises that past hurts and injuries should be remembered and redressed *except when to do so would cause more harm.* This is excellent advice. While I am a big fan of honesty, I also know that there are times when sleeping dogs should be allowed to slumber undisturbed.

We have learned much about the damaging effects of growing up in a so-called "dysfunctional family." Bookshelves have been filled with works on this issue. Let it be enough to say here that, unfortunately, years of tension, drug or alcohol abuse, physical, mental, or sexual abuse, neglect, or other family drama complicates this review of the past for many families. Family Systems experts say that the best families are no more than 60 percent healthy. Still, I believe that it is important to remember the parts of the relationship for which one is thankful even when there are other parts of the relationship that are strained and painful. Also, it is tremendously healing to make an honest acknowledgment of one's anger and resentment over those parts of the relationship that were disappointing, hurtful, or damaging even if you never actually share it.

It is sometimes helpful to ask a third party to help you and your family with your end-of-life review. Working with a counselor, chaplain, or clergyperson skilled in these issues can be a way of creating a safe place for talking about painful or strained memories. If other family members are not interested in joining you in this review of the past, it may be helpful for you to find a therapist or even simply a trusted friend with whom you can share your thoughts and feelings. At the very least, take some time by yourself to sort things out.

4. Keeping Your Sense of Humor

Without a doubt, death is grim business. Loss is not fun. But just because you are dealing with a sad situation, this doesn't mean you can't appreciate, enjoy, and benefit from the lighter moments as they come along.

Some people might disagree with me here. Some believe they should approach death with grim, stoic determination. There should be no joking around. The "death room" should be sterile and somber, quiet and serious. If you believe this way, I respect your beliefs, but I have to say I could not disagree more.

Death and dying is just too sad to take more seriously than absolutely necessary. It is a rare setting in which moments of genuine, heartfelt humor are not profoundly appreciated. I had a parishioner who was in the intensive care unit because of complications of her cancer. For some reason they would not allow her family to visit, but they would allow me, as her pastor, to see her. My visits were generally brief and lighthearted. I would tell her what was going on at the church, pray, and playfully tell her to "Heal fast! We're keeping a pew warm for you." Later she told me how much having someone come by who treated her like a living, breathing human being and not a deathbed patient or a "case" had meant to her.

It is amazing how often simply ridiculous events accompany the experience of dying. Who could resist laughing out loud when the caregiver tripped over the dog and spilled the bedpan all over the cat? Or what about the time an ill-fitting hospital gown caused Uncle Harry to "moon" the entire waiting room? Whose heart would not melt when they saw the cat curled up on Grandma's lap as they both snoozed off the effects of her latest chemotherapy?

One of the gifts of working to create a healing experience of death is to give permission for everyone to appreciate the lighter moments and the simple pleasures that help us get through life's rougher spots. Don't be afraid to smile or even laugh out loud even though you or someone you love is dying. Your laughter is just as much a gift of love as are your tears.

I often hear families apologize for the "sick" inside jokes they use to find relief from the frustrations of dealing with death and dying. This "gallows humor" may sound callous or mean-spirited to those outside the situation, but it may be just the thing that allows those who are caught up in it to talk about things that are otherwise too scary or intense. Many, perhaps most, families who are going through death and dying are known to smile knowingly or work hard to cover a smirk from time to time. There are no limits to the targets of these "attacks." Stuffy, self-important medical personnel, the cold bureaucracy of insurance companies, and the inane rigidity of hospital rules and regulations are all common targets of lampoons. I say, "Let 'em have it!" Take your comic relief wherever you can find it.

Many of us, myself included, have a hard time talking straight up about difficult things. Corny attempts at humor when the pain gets intense or things look dark are a way for us — for me — to talk about the unspeakable. Still, as much as I enjoy a good joke, I also realize that humor should never be used as a shield from true emotion. There is a time to speak directly of serious things. Death is sad and troubling, and we need to express honestly our sadness and upset. Even so, laugh every once in a while. Cut up in the hospital room. Take your pot shots when you can. The tears of a clown speak to the fullness of human emotion and love just as much as the somber tolling of the bell.

Another aspect of humor during death and dying is taking an occasional "time out" on the grief and sadness. Declaring a "no cry zone" from time to time might be just the thing you need to help everyone refresh and regroup. Rent or go out to see a silly movie. Go to a nice restaurant. Take a drive in the country. Sit in the yard. Get your hair or nails done. Participate in a favorite hobby as you are able. Go fishing. Take turns reading a joke book to one another. Play a game. Put a puzzle together. Surf the web. Give yourselves permission to forget your problems for a while.

One of the best stories I ever heard was told to me by a member of one of the churches I served. It was about a trip she made to the hairdresser with her mother and sister. My parishioner, who had emphysema, was wearing her portable oxygen mask and pushing her mother, who had lung disease and was in a wheelchair. Following behind with her hand on her shoulder was my parishioner's sister, who had her eyes bandaged from recent surgery on her corneas. As they slowly stumbled their way into the shop, her sister started singing "Three Blind Mice." As they opened the door, everyone in the hair salon looked and stared. It was not because they were a medical disaster on wheels. It was because they were all three giggling so hard they could hardly walk. The moral: don't worry about what others think. They probably wouldn't understand anyway. Do what you can to put the "fun" back in "funeral."

5. Telling the Truth

Probably one of the most difficult aspects of dealing with death and dying is trying to figure out *who* needs to know *what* and *when*. Many of us take-charge types — I was the big brother, I can't help it — sometimes think that we know what is best for everyone else and like to dole out information when and to whom we deem necessary. This is generally *not* a good way of doing it. No matter how kind we might think we are being by sparing others the burdens of bad news, people need and deserve to know what is going on. A study of hospice families in the 1990s showed that the vast majority of the individuals who were dying indicated that they wanted to know what was going on with them. A similar number of family members wanted to know the truth as well.

Information is power. While family members might want to "spare" or protect one another from painful truth, to keep information from the dying person is to interfere with the process of coming to terms with what is happening. In the same way, to keep information from a loved one will hinder caregiving and support. The Bible says, "The truth will set you free." Telling a dying loved one the truth about the situation provides an opportunity to get affairs in order. Telling the truth to the family allows them to rally their resources and circle their loved one with care. Telling the truth is a special and much appreciated gift. Only by knowing the truth can goodbyes be said and attempts to reconcile old hurts and divisions be made.

There was a time when medical personnel routinely kept "bad news" from the dying and their families. While that is mercifully rare now, it still happens. If your "gut" tells you that someone is withholding information, ask flat out, "Are you telling me everything about this situation?" If you still get the feeling that you are getting the runaround, ask someone else. And keep on asking till you get the information you need. If the doctor won't tell you the truth, talk to the nurse, the therapist, the aide, the lunch person, anybody and everybody. While medical personnel are bound by rules of confidentiality, they are also bound by rules of "informed consent." Don't feel rushed to sign a consent form you don't understand. Ask your questions till your get answers that make sense to you. While medical personnel are often in a hurry, remember that you and your insurance company are paying dearly for a bit of their time. Get your money's worth! Write your questions down as they come to you and keep asking them until you are satisfied with the answers. Seek second and third opinions. Do your own research and be an informed consumer.

Truthtelling is also important between family members and caregivers. I have had people tell me they felt they couldn't tell the truth to one or more family members who were considered too "delicate" or "fragile" to cope with such unpleasant information. Whenever that happens I am reminded of Jack Nicholson's great line in the movie *A Few Good Men.* — "Truth! You can't handle the truth!" While I suppose there are circumstances and conditions where it might be unkind or even dangerous to share bad news with some gentle souls, my inclination is always to err on the side of transparency. Those who have a hard time handling the truth can be dealt with in appropriate and caring ways. But who are you to judge that someone is incompetent to hear something they really need and deserve to hear? In the words of the sage, "Blessed are the transparent, for they shall have nothing to hide."

The Internet is a great source of information on medical conditions, treatment options, and new medications. Just make sure that the source of your information is trustworthy. There are a lot of crackpots pushing lots of crazy ideas on the web. Be wary of miracle cures that sound too good to be true or require you to pay up front for information. Generally, websites associated with government-sponsored research facilities, universities, or large teaching hospitals are reliable. Even then, try to find out who is sponsoring the research trials of a particular drug or treatment that might be of interest to you. Be suspicious of data or research sponsored by a particular drug company. Recent reports have revealed that who is paying for the study often influences what the study finds.

Also, I've heard stories about medical personnel being embarrassed when a patient or family member brings in an article from the Internet describing new research or a treatment they didn't know about. I say, don't worry about their embarrassment. A good doctor will welcome your information. This is your life or the life of someone you love. If it will help, embarrass away!

6. Maintaining a Sense of Self

All too often a terminal diagnosis is interpreted to mean "Sit there quietly until you die." My response is, "Why?" Your dying loved one is still the same person they were before you all got this bit of information. Everyone is dying. Your loved one just happens to know that time is coming sooner rather than later. Why sit like a lump of wet clay when you can all be using whatever time you might have left to grab whatever final gusto is possible? Passively sitting back and waiting for death robs you and your loved one of what joy you might otherwise have had.

You may have years to enjoy together. You may have weeks to enjoy together. Either way, "now" is all the time you have. Live every day to its fullest. As long as you both are still breathing, put that breath to good use. Keep up with friends, activities, work, hobbies, and all the other things that fill life with meaning and joy. Just because someone is dying doesn't mean they are dead! If your loved ones can still get out, get out. If your loved ones can walk, walk; if not, get a wheelchair or an electric scooter. Help your loved ones stay occupied even if they can't do the things they used to do in the way they used to do them. Don't let go of your loved ones until they are dragged kicking and screaming from your life.

If disease or growing weakness makes it hard to do everyday tasks — getting dressed, cooking, getting around the house, eating, etc. — ask to see a physical or occupational therapist for help with issues of mobility or information about adaptive equipment designed to help those who are disabled by their conditions with daily activities. You would be amazed at the variety of specialized devices there are to help with eating, getting dressed, bathing, and other everyday tasks. A speech therapist can help with eating or swallowing concerns or with communication issues. Check to see if your insurance company covers these kinds of expenses. Some churches have access to equipment that they are willing to lend for free or for a minimal donation. Caregivers should take their clue from the person who is dying. If an interest in trying something is expressed, do your best to help them do it.

There was a time when "disabled" and "handicapped" meant the same thing. The word "handicapped" goes back to the days when persons with physical limitations would sit on the sidewalk with cap in hand begging for handouts because society had no use and no room for them. Thankfully those days are long gone. Where it was once rare to see people out and about in a wheelchair or motorized cart, you see them everywhere you go now. Many malls and grocery stores have motorized carts available for patrons at no or low cost. Though it is still controversial in some circles, the Americans with Disabilities Act (ADA) has gone a long way in removing many of the physical and psychological barriers that have kept people with special needs at home. Government buildings, museums, libraries, churches, apartment buildings, parks, theaters, restaurants, malls, business places — almost anywhere you want to go — are now accessible to practically anyone with a physical disability. There is no longer any reason for people to stay at home just because they are no longer as mobile as they used to be. Most cars can be retrofitted with controls to make it possible for many persons with limited strength to continue to drive.

Once again, my message is simple: We all should take charge of our lives for as long as we live. There was once a time when the sight of a person in a wheelchair or using a cane, or a person with a colostomy bag, an oxygen tank, or some other medical appliance would seem out of place in public. That is much less true now than in the past. People used to cover their bald heads to hide the fact they were on chemotherapy. Now the shaved look is hot!

Another part of maintaining one's sense of self is paying attention to personal grooming. Body image is a huge part of self esteem. A glance at any fashion magazine in the grocery store or at the multimillion-dollar diet industry in our country should be enough to convince you that looking good is important to most people. I have talked to people who, though saddened by their terminal illness, were most bothered by the possibility of physical disfigurement. Similarly, family members report that watching the disease process change or restrict a loved one's appearance or activities to be heartbreaking. Often sickroom odors make it unpleasant or embarrassing to feel good about visiting or having people stop by.

I once met a very elegant elderly woman who had been a model in her younger days. All her life she had been surrounded by beauty. She had always dressed in the latest fashion. Even on her deathbed she would not allow anyone into her room until she had had her hair done and her makeup touched up. She usually had a scarf around her neck or draped strategically across the sheets, giving a dash of color, drama, and elegance to an otherwise sterile setting. She didn't care who wanted to see her: doctor, nurse, pastor, or friend. This was her life and her body and she was going to go out as she had always lived: in style! If that meant that visitors and medical personnel had to wait until she was ready to receive them, too bad.

Paying attention to dress, grooming, and mobility is not just vanity. It helps the dying feel more presentable and may help others focus more on the person and less on the disease. Remember, *people* are the bottom line in all this. If a little time and money spent on looking good and getting around can help both the dying and others relate to one another as human beings and less as a condition or a problem to be solved, they are time and money well spent. A nice shower that leaves one feeling fresh and clean can help a person who is sick feel good in spite of the disease. Being neat and clean can also help others to feel more relaxed around someone who is not well. Though it may sound as if I'm contradicting myself, if a well-placed scarf or lap blanket that covers up a scar or a colostomy bag, or a hat or wig that covers up the effects of chemotherapy, or a bit of makeup or a fancy fingernail job helps signal the world, "Hey, I'm still here!" then accessorize away! Whether the person who is sick chooses the "au naturel" look or opts to be more covert, do what it takes to help the person feel comfortable and continue to live life to its fullest for as long as possible.

Taking care of personal grooming is difficult when you are weak or disabled because of disease. In a perfect world there would always be a loved one who is available to help with personal health care needs. Unfortunately, our busy lives often make it difficult to spend enough quality time with our dying loved one to take care of all these needs. If the only time you have to spend with your loved one is tied up with cleaning, meal preparation, personal grooming, laundry, etc., there is even less time to spend together in quality, healing ways. I encourage you to consider hiring a home health aide to help you with some of the routine busywork of housekeeping and basic grooming so that family and friends can spend their limited time with their loved one in more personal and less hurried ways. Check with your insurance carrier or Medicare. You might well be eligible for help. If so, take advantage of it even if it is just for a few hours a day.

If you find that you are ineligible for paid help, perhaps caregivers can find a way to take turns so that one or two people are not inordinately burdened. Even out-of-town family and friends can help. I know one family in which a brother and sister-in-law who lived in another state arranged to take care of his mother two weekends a month as she was dying so that the other brothers and sisters and their spouses could take some time for themselves. Was it inconvenient for them to drive several hours twice a month? Yes, it was. Was it worth it to them? Absolutely! Would they do it again? In a heartbeat!

7. Offering Physical and Emotional Expressions of Caring

I'll say it one more time: *people* are what count. Physical and emotional expressions of caring — hugs, kisses, caresses, holding hands, sharing tears —

are, for many of us, the people-to-people connection that makes a healing experience of death possible. But what constitutes an appropriate expression of caring is not always obvious. Some people are comfortable with touching. Some are not. What is important is that each person's emotional response to the situation be respected and valued even if it is not someone else's cup of tea. Both tears and a "stiff upper lip" can be appropriate responses to loss *if* they are honest expressions of that person's personality and emotional state. A hug and kiss may be very welcome at a certain time and place from the right person, but they may be unwelcome and even inappropriate at another time or from another person.

Some people are afraid to express themselves at the time of death and dying because they are afraid that if they get emotional they will "break down" and embarrass themselves. But physical and emotional expressions of caring are not about looking "weak" or "strong" in the face of death and dying. It is not a question of weakness or strength. It is a question of connecting. It is about healing when a cure is not possible. Healing might mean risking shedding a tear even if that is out of character for you. Healing might mean being the one others lean on when you've always thought of yourself as the needy one. I've often seen someone who others feel to be "strong" have to rely on someone who is thought of as "weak" over the course of their experience of death and dying. None of us is *simply* "weak" or *always* "strong." We are *all* capable of being both strong *and* weak depending on the circumstances in which we find ourselves. Trust yourself and your heart to let you know what is appropriate and when.

So often I hear people apologizing for crying when the sadness of death and grief overwhelms them. Our culture, unlike some others, teaches that we're not supposed to cry in public. It is not considered "polite." The old proverb "Big boys don't cry" is still operative in spite of the fact that men have been encouraged to get in touch with their feminine side for more than thirty years. There is an unwritten rule in our culture that says we should keep all strong emotions to ourselves lest we cause someone around us to feel uncomfortable. Too often people worry about "falling apart" in public or in front of friends and family. But I want to suggest that "falling apart" is no more an expression of weakness than "keeping it together" is an expression of strength. Either can be a phony cover-up of what is really going on inside the person's heart. The important thing is that our expression of caring is sincere and meaning-filled. Our tears and our strength are both gifts of love, emotions that should be expressed freely and without shame.

A word of caution, however, about tears. Tears can be used to manipulate others. Both men and women use tears this way. In the same way, gruff, tough acts of machismo by either men or women can also be hollow attempts to bully others away before they get too emotionally close. In either case, death and dying is not the time for playing games. If you feel you want to cry, cry. If you don't feel like crying, don't. But don't use this highly emotional time to try to take advantage of the emotional vulnerability of those around you by either weeping uncontrollably no matter what is going on or by trying to convince others — and yourself — that you are too strong to be caught crying.

People don't connect only through words or tears. We touch. We are touched. It is quite common for dying persons to crave human contact, particularly when they feel they are physically unattractive. Touching, stroking, hugging, holding a hand, a kiss, or brushing the hair can communicate volumes when words fail. It is fairly well established now that even people in comas know of and can benefit from simple human touch. Also, those whose illness has robbed them of their ability to communicate verbally may find touching to be their only means of speaking what is in their heart.

Physical expressions of caring may also involve sexual expressions of love between people who have a physical relationship. I've heard people talk about how one last opportunity to make love was a significant part of their saying goodbye to a spouse of many years. All I can say is: Do what feels right to you. Ask your doctor if you are worried that sexual contact or excitement might be hurtful or damaging to the dying person. If intercourse itself is no longer possible, you might experiment with other forms of sexual contact that are pleasurable and meaningful to both of you.

8. Seeking the Presence of Significant Others

Finally, *the single most important factor in creating a healing experience of death is the presence of important friends and family.* Nothing can convey love and caring at the end of one's life like the physical presence of those who made life most worthwhile. Spending quality time at the bedside of their loved one assures those who survive that they did everything they could. Not only the dying but also those who provide care for them need the energy and love family and friends bring.

People often feel awkward about visiting someone who is sick and dying. They worry, "What will we do? What will we talk about? What if I say the 'wrong thing'?" You don't have to worry about having the right thing to do or say when you visit your dying loved one. Just be yourself as you have always been with them. It is your presence and your time that are most important. Talk about the same things you always talked about together. Talk about golf or football. Talk about how your garden is doing. Share the latest gossip. Talk about the kids. Show off your pictures. Play cards. Often doing and talking are not even necessary. Sometimes just watching TV or a movie together is all that is needed. Tell them how much their friendship has meant to you. Sometimes it is nice to just sit in the yard and enjoy the sunshine with someone you care about.

Sometimes it is difficult to be in the presence of a dying friend or family member, particularly if there have been significant physical changes since the last visit — the loss or gain of a lot of weight, the loss of hair, a dramatic decline in energy, an increased reliance on walkers or wheelchairs to get around, the presence of scars or bandages, etc. It may fall to the dying person to start the conversation or to let visitors know they don't mind talking about being sick. Other family or friends who are more used to the changes can often ease the awkwardness by initiating "safe" topics of conversation. Once visitors know that this is still their same old friend, they will usually relax, and both can get on with the business of being human with each other.

Also, people are often reluctant to initiate a visit with someone who is terminally ill because they don't want to "bother" them, or "disrupt the routine." Again, it may be up to the dying person or a close caregiver to call and invite them over. If your dying loved one expresses interest in seeing someone, give that person a call. Make a date. Dash off a note or an e-mail. If you hear that someone you know is dying, take the initiative to invite yourself over. The awkwardness will last for only a short while, but the memories of your time together will last forever.

Often those who are dying get to feeling ignored, as if they are dead before they are dead. I attribute this to a desire on the part of family and friends not to burden someone who is not feeling well with silly, mundane matters. But being included in boring, everyday events and discussions is what lets us know we are still a part of the living and have not been pushed aside and forgotten! Include dying family members in small talk and family gossip. Get their opinion on what you should wear and what to prepare for dinner. Get their vote on what movie to rent for Friday night and what to put on the Saturday night pizza.

Family members and friends who are serving as home caregivers also need the presence and support of friends and family. It is wonderful to be asked, "And how are *you* doing?" when you have been up to your ears in caring for someone else for weeks. If you are a friend or family member who cannot be a regular part of the caregiving team, volunteer to sit with the person needing care while the regular caregiver slips out for a while. "Hijack" the caregiver off to dinner and a movie while someone stays at the bedside. This can feel like a two-week vacation and will be *much* appreciated. If you are the caregiver and people ask, "What can I do to helpful?" take them up on their offer and give them something to do.

Sometimes our obligations make spending time together difficult or impossible. Families are scattered all over the country and world. It is not unusual for parents and children to be separated by hundreds of miles. Military obligations or educational or employment opportunities may take family members away. Some family members may even be incarcerated and unable to go home. Sometimes family members or friends are sick themselves and no longer able to travel. All I can say is, Do what you can. We have wonderful technological tools available now to help us "reach out and touch someone." Phone calls, e-mail, video webcasting, cassette tapes, videotapes, even old fashioned pen and paper letters are all ways to be there when you can't be there. If you are not a "techie" yourself, ask around and see if you can find someone who can wire you up.

As noted above, some family relationships have been strained to the breaking point by tension, abuse, drug and alcohol use, or some other dysfunction. This, of course, complicates being with the ones you love, as the ones you love may not love one another. Also, family issues may have resulted in some family members being cut off from the main family with little or no contact between the two groups for years.

Still, if you are dying or hear that someone who was once important in your life is dying, it may be worth trying for at least a temporary reconciliation. If you have not been in contact for a number of years, it might be best to ease back into contact slowly. A letter followed by a phone call followed by an exchange of pictures followed by a low expectation visit in a safe, neutral place may need to precede an actual in-home visit. Schedule your first visit to be short, and then lengthen it if and when it feels safe to do that. Don't expect to redress an entire lifetime's hurts in one meeting. These encounters seldom go as smoothly as in the movies, but that doesn't mean it is not worth making an attempt to see if some resolution is possible. Ease yourselves back into contact with one another. Don't try to rush or force matters.

Sometimes divorce can put the children of that divorce in an awkward position if the care needs of a dying parent make the other parent jealous of the extra time the child is spending with a former spouse. Being a child of divorce myself, I know that all you can do is feel your way through the situation carefully. First, get it clear in your own mind what you want to do. If you want to be involved with your dying parent's care, find a way to gently, but firmly, let your other parent know that that's the way it is going to be. Love is not a zero-sum game. Spending more time with one parent at a time of particular need does not detract from the love you have for your other parent. Also, the death of a former spouse may trigger all kinds of feelings in a person who thought that divorce had closed that chapter of his or her life. It might be very kind for you to ask your living parent what he or she thinks and feels about a former spouse passing away.

Chapter Seven

Healing Together

Issues Raised in Chapter Six

We have considered eight strategies for creating healing when a cure is no longer possible. I encourage you now to go back through chapter 6 and consider whether there is a natural spot for you to begin customizing these strategies for yourself. It is likely you are already following some of these suggestions. There may be other possibilities that make you nervous just thinking about them.

Again, remember: there is no *one* way to do this. When it comes to death, dying, and grief we are *all* amateurs and we are *all* experts. Take your time. Breathe deeply. Pray. Then jump on in. Make your mistakes, regroup, then jump back in again.

Death is not easy. Grief is hard work. But both are natural, God-given elements of our lives. We need not be ashamed or afraid of either. Giving attention to these eight areas of concern will make your helping the one you love experience death much easier and will assist you in your work of grief.

◆ ◆ ◆

It is by working *together* in an emotionally honest way and taking charge of the things you can handle that you create a healing experience of death even when cure is not possible. I've also emphasized that the primary player in all this is the person who is dying. So the first thing you are going to do is get as many of this person's wishes down on paper as possible.

Sit down, perhaps just the two of you or perhaps with one or two others — a spouse or significant other, or a child or grandchild who is particularly close; someone who can help to create a loving, supportive, safe environment. Using the questions found in this chapter, go through the various strategies one by one. Again, there is no one place to start. For me the natural place to start is at the beginning with "Paying Attention to the Details of Dying." You might want to start somewhere else if that feels more comfortable. If you hit a question that doesn't seem to have an answer, skip it and go on to something else. You can always go back and fill in the blanks later.

The idea here is to help set the stage by letting the dying person describe what should or should not happen. Don't worry about "getting it right" the first time through. Expect to make revisions and modifications as the process unfolds. Remember the secret to success: flexibility. You will be writing in pencil or at most in pen, *not* in stone or blood. Nothing you write down should be considered unchangeable *unless* the person who is dying says it is.

Please *do not* try to work through all these questions in one or two marathon sessions. That would be simply overwhelming. Also, you may need to set this book down from time to time to do a little digging to find some of the information you are looking for. Some of the information, for example, how to apply for veteran's burial benefits, can be obtained from your funeral director or the nearest VA center. Details on your spiritual tradition's practices can be gotten from your pastor or a hospital or hospice chaplain. Addresses and phone numbers of important people to be contacted or friends to be notified may need to be collected from a variety of sources. It may take a little digging to locate and collect all the financial and insurance information you will want to have together. If possible, it is a good idea to assign specific tasks to certain persons in order to make the job less of a burden on one or two individuals.

Please *do* give yourselves permission to stop from time to time to take a deep breath and share a tear or a giggle. You might want to set a timer or plan to work for only a short stretch at a time — say thirty or forty-five minutes. Expect the conversations to be emotionally trying, but also emotionally rewarding. Watch for the emergence of dysfunctional roles as old buttons get pushed with regard to certain sensitive topics. Do what you can to stick to tasks and functions.

Before you start through the strategies, though, consider first where you are right now. What notions of death, dying, and grief do you bring to this task? Do your existing ideas hold together to help you make sense of what you are about to attempt, or do you find yourself wrestling with contradictory advice? As you begin to build this atmosphere of healing, think for a few minutes about what you have already learned or been told about death, dying, and grief.

- What kind of advice on dealing with death and dying have you gotten?

- What of what you have heard makes sense to you?

- What of what you have heard does *not* make sense to you?

- What do you anticipate will be the hardest part of creating a healing atmosphere?

- What resources (books, people, finances, etc.) can you draw on?

- Which family members, friends, or neighbors might be of help?

- Which family member, friends, or neighbors might get in your way?

- What can you do and who can you turn to if you need help dealing with a family member, friend or neighbor who gets in the way of creating a healing experience of death?

In chapter 6 I listed eight strategies for creating a healing experience of death. The following questions are designed to address the issues raised by these strategies. These questions (pages 92–103) are addressed primarily to the dying person. Caregivers can also respond as is appropriate.

1. Paying Attention to the Details of Death and Dying

These questions will help you think about how you are working with your medical team.

* Are medical personnel respectful of your and your loved one's wishes?
* Do they listen to and answer *all* your questions?
* If not, who can you turn to for answers?
* Who is the one person who is particularly helpful to you?
* Who else do you find is helpful?
* Who is *not* helpful to you?
* Do medical personnel get back to you in timely manner when they say they will?
* Who can you talk to if things are not going according to your wishes?
* Do you want to live your last days at the hospital or care facility, or at home?
* Will you have hospice help?
* If so, who will be your primary hospice contact person?
* What kinds of "heroic measures" would you like to have performed?

  – Intubation

  – Heart defibrillation

  – Artificial hydration

  – Artificial nutrition

  – An NG tube

  – A "peg" tube

* What about medications?

  – Pain medication

  – Morphine

  – Other medication

- Other medical measures
- Do you have a DNR (Do Not Resuscitate) order?
- Have you signed a Living Will? Does your medical team have a copy of it?
- Do all the people who may be with you at the moment of death know your wishes?
- Do you have a "DO NOT CALL 911 (EMS)" sign on all the phones?
- Do you have a "DO NOT CALL 911 (EMS)" sign over the bed?

Death and dying bring with them a host of legal and financial questions and concerns. Failure to get these matters straightened out will cause no end of headaches for those left behind. The following questions can be helpful in getting the necessary legal and financial information organized.

- Where are your birth and marriage certificates? If you cannot find them, where can you get duplicates?
- Who is your lawyer? Name? Address? Phone number?
- Do you have a Last Will and Testament?
    - Where is it?
    - When was the last time it was updated?
    - Who is your executor?
- Do you have a Durable Power of Attorney for Health Care?
    - Who have you named as your spokesperson?
    - If you do not have a Durable Power of Attorney for Health Care, who do you trust to speak for you when the time comes you cannot speak for yourself?
- Do you have a Durable Power of Attorney for other (financial) issues? Who have you named as your POA?
- What survivors' benefits are available and who is named in your insurance policies?

   – Who will receive benefits?

   – Have you titled cars, real estate, boats, etc. in such a way that the transfer of ownership to survivors will be quick and easy?

   – Has your executor or other survivor signed signature cards or other documents at the bank or other institutions so they will have access to your accounts, insurance, etc.?

- Where are your titles, insurance policies, tax records, etc. located?

- Where is your safe deposit box located? Where is the key? What is the password?

- What is your social security number?

- What computer accounts do you have and what are the addresses, log-on names, and passwords for each?

   – Unsecured accounts (e.g., email, AOL, etc.)

   – Secured accounts (e.g., bank accounts, eBay, etc.)

- For the following list all the necessary account information: Account name; account number, institution, address, phone number

   – Savings

   – Checking

   – CDs

   – IRAs

   – Retirement accounts

   – Veterans' benefits

   – Life insurance

   – Car insurance

   – Homeowner's insurance

   – Pension plan

   – Safe deposit box

- Who is your accountant/tax preparer? Name? Address? Phone number?
- Where are your vehicle registrations and titles located?
- Where are your mortgage or rental papers?
- Who manages your stock portfolio? Name? Address? Phone number?
- What other financial records or concerns need to be addressed?
- Are your medical bills in order? Who is handling this? Who will handle future bills?
- Are your personal bills in order? Who will handle them when you are no longer able?

Distributing personal items after a death can be emotionally trying. The distribution of cash and items of great value should be included in your will. Consider here what you would like to have done with items not mentioned in your will. List the individual items and the person to whom they should go. Any leftover items can be assigned to a charity you name.

Your funeral or memorial service is the last opportunity for friends and family to say good-bye and to share their grief together. These questions will help you think about your funeral or memorial plans.

- Would you like to donate your body or parts of your body to science or for organ transplantation?

  - What institution(s) would you like to donate to?
  - What organs would you like to donate?
  - Does the funeral director and hospital know that you want to donate your body or body parts?

- Would you like to be buried or cremated?

  - If you would like to be buried, where would you like to be buried?
  - What kind of casket would you like? Wooden? If so, what kind of wood? Metal? If so what color would you like it to be painted?
  - If you would like to be cremated, what would you like to have done with your ashes?

- Would you prefer a funeral (held right after the death) or a memorial (held some weeks after the death)?

  - Where would you like to have your service held (funeral home, your place of worship, or some other place)?

  - Rather than a funeral, would you prefer a simple graveside service?

  - Would you prefer no service at all?

- Which funeral home would you like to work with?

  - Name? Address? Phone number? Contact person?

  - Do you have a prepaid funeral plan?

- What place of worship would you like to be notified? Name? Address? Phone number? Contact person?

- Regarding the service itself:

  - Who would you like to speak at your funeral or memorial?

  - What music would you like to have played?

  - What songs would you like to have sung?

  - What musician or singers would you like to perform?

  - Which hymns would you like to have sung?

  - Which scriptures or other religious readings would you like to have read?

  - What CDs or videos would you like to have played?

  - Do you want flowers?

  - If yes, what kinds of flowers would you like?

  - What should happen to the flowers after the funeral?

  - Where should memorial gifts be directed?

  - What kind of casket (for burial) or urn (for cremation) would you like?

  - How would you like to be dressed?

- What would you like to have with you in the casket (jewelry, pictures, mementos, etc.)?

- Who would you like to serve as your pallbearers?

♦ What would you like to have on your headstone?

♦ If you are a veteran, would you like to have military honors? If so, please provide the following information.

- Pension or VA number

- Service serial number

- Branch of the service in which you served

- Highest grade or rank

- Unit in which you served

- War or conflict in which you served

- Decorations, medals, or honors

- Would you like a flag?

- Would you like a veteran's cemetery marker?

♦ Are you a member of a club, professional organization, lodge, or fraternal order that has funeral rites? Would you like to have them performed? If so, who should be contacted? Organization? Address? Phone number? Contact person?

♦ Would you like to have an obituary in the newspaper?

- If so, which newspaper(s)? Newspaper, Address, Phone number, Contact person

- Please list your next of kin

- Spouse (former spouse)

- Siblings and their spouses

- Children

- Grandchildren

- Great grandchildren

- Parents (if still living)

- Clubs, professional organizations, fraternal orders, etc.

- Education: high school, college degree, post-graduate degree

- Work history and professional accomplishments

- Significant life events

2. Talking about Religious Issues and Exploring the Afterlife

♦ Have you asked about or seemed preoccupied with questions of death and afterlife?

♦ Have you or others been asking, "Why is this happening?"

♦ Do you feel helpless or cheated?

♦ What do you feel thankful for?

♦ Are you angry with God? Life? Yourself?

♦ Have your children or grandchildren been asking religious questions?

♦ What do you think happens after you die?

♦ What do you think heaven is like?

♦ If God loves us, why would God allow us to die?

♦ Who might you talk with about these kinds of issues?

♦ Has your pastor or other religious leader visited?

♦ Would you like your pastor or religious leader to visit?

♦ If you don't have a pastor or religious leader, would you like to talk with a chaplain or a nearby pastor?

- Have you been attending religious services?

- If not, would you like to go?

- Where would you like to go?

- Who could take you?

- Do you have a copy of your religious tradition's scriptures? If not, would you like a copy?

- What would you like to ask God right now?

- What is particularly satisfying about your spiritual or religious practice these days?

- What would make your spiritual or religious practice more satisfying?

3. Reviewing Your Life's Story

- What holidays or family celebrations are coming up when you can gather everyone together?

- Who would you like to see?

- Where are the photo albums or videotapes kept?

- Have you had a chance to go through them?

- What do the children say they will miss when the death occurs?

- What are your fondest memories?

- What are your proudest accomplishments?

- What would you like to be remembered for?

- What was the one thing you regret never getting to do?

- What issues are too emotionally "hot" for you to bring up with certain family members?

- How and with whom might you express these thoughts and feelings?

4. Keeping Your Sense of Humor

- When was the last time you had a really good laugh?

- Have you laughed today?

- What steps are you taking for personal rest and renewal?

- When do you take "time off" from death and dying?

- Who can you call on when you need a break?

- What are you going to do with your time off to make sure it really is time off?

- Heard any good jokes lately?

- What was the funniest story you ever heard?

- Who or What are the "silver linings" in your clouds these days?

- What could you thank God for right now?

- What funny movies would you like to see?

- What has been the funniest medical mess-up this week?

- Who has looked at you as if you were totally insane this week? Why?

- Are there serious things that need to be said but are being hidden behind an attempt to look cheerful?

5. Telling the Truth

- Does everybody involved with this situation know everything the others know?

- Do you have a sense there is someone who wants to know something, but isn't asking?

- Which of your questions are not being answered?

- Are you keeping secrets?

- Who are you keeping secrets from and why?

- Is your medical team playing straight with you?

- Who in your circle is "too fragile" to handle the truth about what is happening?

- Who is going to tell anyway?

- What are you going to do if tears start falling?

- What Internet resources are you using for information?

- How well do you trust these sites?

- What alternate sites have you checked?

- What other sources of information (libraries, other professionals, etc.) have you tried?

6. Maintaining a Sense of Self — Active Waiting

- Are you reluctant to have visitors because of the way you look?

- Are you wearing your favorite color?

- Which is your favorite shirt? Pants? Skirt? Dress?

- Which are your favorite PJs?

- Would a hat, scarf, wig, makeup, etc. make you feel less self-conscious?

- Is there any odor that might be noticeable to visitors?

- What are you doing for fun?

- Where would you like to go today?

- What would you like to do today?

- Are you getting out of the house as much as possible?

- Have you checked out the large print and books on tape/CD section of the library or bookstore?

- Which of the movies that are out now would you like to see?

- What videos would you like to see?

- Are you still engaged in hobbies and activities you have always enjoyed?

- If not, what would enable you to enjoy them again?

- What equipment (wheelchair, cane, walker, etc.) do you need to help you get out of the house?

- What equipment (special spoons, cups, reaching tools, etc.) would make your life easier?

- Would an augmentative communications device or hearing aid make communication easier?

- If you are being cared for at home, how could you check into getting a home health aide?

7. Offering Physical and Emotional Expressions of Caring

• Are you able to touch or hold each other?

• Are you taking turns being "strong" and "weak?"

• How are you feeling?

• Do the others around you know how you are feeling?

• Are you sure?

• Have you taken time to cry and have you allowed others to see your tears?

• Are you being honest with your tears?

• Are you concerned about your own or someone else's emotional well-being?

• If so, what might you do about this?

• Do you still touch?

  – If not, why not?

  – What would make touching more comfortable?

• Do you allow yourself to be touched?

  – If not, why not?

  – What would make being touched more comfortable?

For couples:

• Have you had a chance to be sexually intimate?

• What still "works" for you sexually?

• Have you talked with your doctor about what is still sexually possible?

8. Seeking the Presence of Significant Others

• Who needs to be notified about what is going on? Names? Phone numbers?

• Are you providing opportunities for significant others to be involved?

- Are regular caregivers taking advantage of the visits of family and friends to slip away for their own renewal?

- What games, puzzles, books, videos, etc. do you have that can help "lubricate" awkward moments with visitors?

- Are you still feeling involved in everyday events?

- How are you using technology to stay in touch with family and friends?

- Who could help you with any remaining communication problems?

- With whom can you share your thoughts and feelings?

- Are there misunderstandings, hard feelings, or broken relationships that need to be addressed before it is too late?

- Who could you get to help your family talk about some of the issues they are trying to avoid?

- Who would you like to see or talk with right now?

Chapter Eight

If All This Seems Impossible
Family Dysfunction and Dying

My Family Could Never do This!

By this point, some of you are thinking to yourselves, "This all *sounds* nice, but *my* family could never pull this off in a million years. My family is too (*a*) crazy, (*b*) scattered, (*c*) dysfunctional, (*d*) out of control, (*e*) hateful, (*f*) addicted, or (*g*) all the above, to ever come together in such an honest, open, vulnerable way. I guess this doesn't apply to me. My family will never find healing in death."

Believe me, I know what you are talking about.

As I mentioned above, my Dad died when I was in my mid-twenties. What I didn't mention is that his death occurred several years after my parents' rather messy divorce. Mine was a classic dysfunctional family. By the time Dad got cancer and died, each of my parents had been remarried — my father more than once. My brothers, both of whom had been married and divorced at least once by then, were battling with alcohol and substance abuse. I, meanwhile, had flown the coop at age eighteen and escaped to college and graduate school. Moving out of state, I built a life for myself as far away from home as I could, having come to the unconscious decision that distance was the best way of protecting myself from being hurt by them anymore.

We had never been a particularly close family, even when we were all still at home. By the time Dad got sick, I was doing my best to get home for a few days each year around the holidays. My brothers and I hadn't all been together in the same room for years. We would go for months without contacting one another and when we did it was usually only to pass on critical family news — a birth, a death, a marriage, etc. I was in touch with Mom only sporadically.

With all our break-ups and moving-ons, our addictions and escaping over the border, my family had a hard time talking about even pleasant things. It was impossible to imagine how we'd ever be able to get along well enough to handle something as painful and emotionally charged as helping my father die well.

In fact, we didn't handle it well at all. As embarrassing as it is to admit, not even I, the religious professional, the pastor and counselor, was particularly helpful or available when my father was dying and needed me.

Part of my reason for writing this is to help you avoid some of the mistakes we made. After coming clean with myself about how poorly I did as a son when my father needed me, I began to study and learn from families who did know how to work together. Much of what appears in the previous chapters comes from that research.

What follows is help for the rest of us who come from families that don't know how to work together very well. I will be borrowing here from the work of several authors and teachers who are experts in what is known as "Family Systems Theory." Systems Theory is, to my mind, the most helpful way of understanding the dynamics of families who have difficulties working together during stressful times. It is, for the most part a "no fault" theory of human interaction which suggests that blame for family problems lies in the way interactions and communications have become manipulative and dishonest. It does not assign blame to individual family members or certain traumatic events.

Family Systems suggests that it is more important to focus on function-ing well in the here and now than to try to find reasons from the past for why your family is so messed up. You are perfectly welcome to delve into more analytical forms of intervention if you want, of course, but that will typically take years and cost thousands of dollars in intense therapy. What I will be presenting here is a way for you to take immediate action to handle the situation of death and dying that is at your doorstep today.

A Personal Word on Family Dysfunction

I grew up during the so-called "golden age" of television. The 1950s and 1960s was the era of the variety show (*Ed Sullivan, Carol Burnett*), Westerns (*Wagon Train, Bonanza, Have Gun Will Travel*), and, who could forget, the situation comedy. The sit-coms of this era were often family based (*Ozzie and Harriet, Donna Reed, Father Knows Best, My Three Sons, Leave It to Beaver,* etc.) and they followed a familiar pattern. Mom was always beautiful, immaculately groomed with pearls and high heels, and totally devoted to her family's needs. Dad was a handsome devil who wore a suit and tie to the office, always had time for his family, and seemed to have the answers for all life's problems. Brother and sisters squabbled, but always stood up for each other when the chips were down. Pets always did what they were told to do — unless their misbehavior helped move the plot along. There were seldom any worries about money, and even when there were money problems, they never threatened the very stability of the family itself. No one ever got seriously hurt. No one died. No one cussed, or walked out or told anybody off. No one cheated on his or her marriage. No one was ever physically, emotionally, or sexually abused. The only one who drank too much was the lovable town drunk. No one gambled away the rent money. And, most important of all, *all* problems were solved in thirty minutes or less.

I enjoyed the variety shows when my parents let me stay up late enough to see them. I loved the Westerns and spent long hours reenacting their cowboy-and-Indian sagas in the back yard with my friends. I know that's not politically correct today, but it was after all the 1950s. But I *hated* the sit-coms. Even though I might find something in a particular episode amusing, they left me feeling bad. Even as a kid, I knew there was something fundamentally phony about these happy little everything-comes-out-in-the-end shows. What bothered me about them was that they portrayed a family life that was completely false. They pretended to be real, but they weren't.

Real parents weren't always smiling and loving. Real siblings didn't always stand up for each other. Real dogs peed on the floor. Neglect and abuse happened. Real families fought over sex and money. Sometimes people left and never came back. Real parents sometimes said terrible things to each other and sometimes dinner ended up on the floor. Real mothers weren't always beautiful and well groomed, nor did they have plates of hot cookies waiting when you got home from school. Sometimes they weren't there when you got home, and sometimes even when they were home they couldn't care less that you were. Real dads sometimes drank too much, or worked longer than they had to. They didn't have all the answers to life's questions and sometimes they made you feel stupid for asking. In real life, families bickered and fought. In real life, family members hurt and used each other. In real life, families sometimes split up. In real life, people got sick and hurt and sometimes they died.

As I watched these shows, I remember a growing sense that there was something terribly wrong with my family. We didn't seem to match the picture of ideal family life that was broadcast each night on Channel 3. Later, when my parents split up, their divorce was in some way the confirmation of my fears. Like many kids growing up in the first TV generation, I came to the earth-shattering realization that real life and sit-com life were not the same and that it was somehow *my* family's fault that we didn't measure up.

The reason I mention this is that as some of you read about coming together as family and friends to love and support one another as you build a healing space in the face of death and dying, you too may be feeling the same queasy, unreal feelings I felt watching the 1950s and '60s sitcoms. Without any real-life experience to suggest that families *can* actually work together, you don't believe it is possible. Maybe Ozzie and Harriet or the Cleavers or the Huxtables could muster the energy and honesty and love to pull off coming together to find healing, but my family? You've got to be kidding!

None of Us Is from a Perfect Family

Let's take a moment to reflect on your particular situation. How do you honestly feel about yourself and your relationship with your family? Do you feel as if there are eggshells under your feet when you are around certain members of your family? Does it feel safe to visit, disagree with, or even talk on the phone with all the members of your family? Do you have to "psych yourself up" before you can be around certain family members? Are there some members of your family who give you the creeps and who you try to avoid being alone with? Does there always have to be alcohol around whenever your family gathers? Are there certain topics that your family simply avoids at all costs — the so called "elephants in the living room"? Are there certain members of your family who have chosen to be absent from family events most of the time? Do some family members always try to control or "fix" the others? Do some members of your family seem to be clueless, "broken," or just plain "lost" most of the time?

If you said "yes" to one or more of these questions, you grew up in a less than perfect family. Welcome to the human race. The fact is that most families are less than perfect. Family Systems experts suggest that even the healthiest families are only about 60 percent healthy, leaving even the best families with a lot of room for less-than-perfection.

Most families have problems. Most of us grew up looking at other families and thinking, "Gee, I wish I lived with them." The truth probably is that they were looking at our family thinking the same thing.

"Family dysfunction" is a term that is being used to describe the less-than-perfect reality most of us grew up in. Dysfunctional families do all the same things other families do, but where some families seem to function with ease and good humor, dysfunctional families seem to operate with a lot of barely controlled pain. Some dysfunctional families are dysfunctional about everything. Other dysfunctional families seem to be able to handle most situations well but fall apart around certain subjects or events. Some dysfunctional families are obviously dangerous with physical, emotional, or sexual abuse or active alcohol or drug use going on day after day. Some family dysfunction shows up as divorce, teen pregnancy, loud fighting, chronic financial worries, or unexplained bruises, burns, and black eyes. But, much family dysfunction is less obvious. It shows up as kids who never seem to be able to grow up and leave home, or as interfering parents who never seem to be able to let their kids live their own lives. Sometimes family dysfunction shows up in cute T-shirt truisms — "Momma ain't happy, ain't nobody happy!" Some family dysfunction is obvious and ugly. Some is sickly, seductively sweet in a false, unreal Norman-Rockwell-on-steroids kind of way.

Whole bookshelves have been written on the topic of family dysfunction. A trip to a good library or bookstore would be worthwhile if you want to know more than what I am going to go into here. The reason I am talking about it is that family dysfunction often complicates the experience of death, dying, and grief. While the occasion of death can bring out the *best* in some families as they rally together to cope with a difficult time, it can also bring out the *worst* in other families as the added stress of death overwhelms the delicate dysfunctional ways of relating to one another they count on to keep themselves going. Growing up in a dysfunctional family tends to make us less able to build the kind of network we would like to have to support our loved one as death draws near. Growing up in a dysfunctional family makes it hard for us to have the kinds of honest heart-to-heart conversations and to follow through with the kinds of commitments I've been encouraging you to have. So, if we are ever going to come together to find healing when a cure is no longer possible, we've got to first get a handle on dysfunction and see how we can work around it to reach our goal of a healing experience of death.

A Primer on Family Dysfunction

What I am going to present here are just the basics of Family Systems Theory and how it applies to the issue of dealing with death and dying.

Other authors may use different terms to describe some of these concepts, but I think you'll find that what follows is pretty much mainstream.

1. Pressure, pressure, pressure

Family dysfunction begins with the experience of *chronic anxiety*. Other authors may call it chronic stress or chronic conflict. Whatever you call it, chronic anxiety is the universal human experience of the unresolved and the irresolvable tension between what "is" and what "ought" to be.

Chronic anxiety can look like a woman who feels she is a bad mother because she doesn't measure up to the ideal she carries with her as memories — often exaggerated or downright false — of her own "perfect" mother. Chronic anxiety can look like my reaction to years of feeling inferior to the "perfect" families on the sit-coms of my youth. Chronic anxiety can look like an adult child who senses that no matter what she does, she has always been and will always be a disappointment to her parents. It can look like a man who has been told all his life that he is never going to amount to anything, and sure enough, he doesn't. Chronic anxiety can be the result of societal prejudice and injustices with regard to race, gender, or sexual orientation. Chronic anxiety can be the result of growing up in the chaotic world of a home where alcohol or drugs were abused, or where physical, sexual, or emotional abuse or neglect occurred. Chronic anxiety has a million faces, all of which are unpleasant. As it has permeated our entire society, chronic anxiety is what gives power to Wall Street advertisements that play on our desires to be smarter, sexier, more youthful, more successful, or in some other way a happier, more satisfied human.

Some of you may be thinking that the tension between what is and what ought to be is a good thing. As destructive as stress and anxiety can be, there are some people who seem to thrive on them or at least who can use the tension between what is and what ought to be for positive ends. Outstanding athletes, for example, motivate themselves by striving to realize the ideal they seek. They push themselves to overcome the gap between their present skills and what they want to achieve. The same could be said about artists, musicians, and other successful professionals and business people. I once read that what motivated Alexander Graham Bell to tinker with electronic communication was his desire to find a way to overcome his wife's hearing disability.

The fact is that a little anxiety is actually good for you. It is anxiety in the form of hunger (or having to go to the bathroom) that gets you out of bed in the morning. It is anxiety in the form of wanting to provide for our families that sends us to work each day. It is anxiety in the form of personal ambition or the desire to serve others that motivates certain persons to achieve great ends.

But when anxiety becomes chronically overwhelming or we believe ourselves to be helpless or hopeless in the face of our anxieties, they can become debilitating. When our anxieties drive us to compare ourselves unfavorably with others, and our sense of self-esteem and self-worth suffer, then chronic anxiety can become an internal demon that binds us to our fears and keeps us from experiencing joy, spontaneity, and grace.

When chronic anxiety becomes unbearable, people seek to compensate through various means. Addictions are one way of handling chronic anxiety. People use alcohol, drugs, sex, gambling, eating, pornography, shopping, complaining, or some other "mood altering" substance or behavior to take their minds off their sense of inadequacy at not being able to handle the things that make them feel bad about themselves. Some authors call this attempt to handle unpleasant feelings of inadequacy through the compulsive use of chemicals or repeated behaviors, "self-medication." They suggest that people use substances or compulsive behaviors to "numb" themselves to the pain of their anxiety.

The trouble with mood altering, of course, is that reality keeps barging in when the effect of our "drug" of choice wear off. Also, as we become more used to our mood altering substance or behavior, it loses its ability to take our mind off what is making us feel bad about ourselves. This leads to the familiar self-destructive spiral where someone addicted to a substance or behavior has to participate in their diversion more and more frequently and at higher and higher doses to get the desired sense of relief.

Other people try to handle their chronic anxiety though trying to take physical or emotional control of the world around them. In its most dramatic form, this can present itself as physical, sexual, or emotional abuse or neglect. It can also take the form of keeping an emotional — and sometimes physical — distance from others. It may look like trying to run someone's life for them. It can take the form of chronic nagging, crankiness, moodiness, "having a fit," "the silent treatment," arguing over anything and everything, slamming doors, threats, drinking binges, being "helpful" when help is not needed or wanted, or one of thousands of other ways we attempt to force others to do what we want them to do. Curiously, it can also look like "cluelessness" where a person tries to control others by never seeming to be able to get their life together so that they constantly need someone to keep track of them. It can sometimes look like more than one of these at the same time.

In whatever form it manifests itself, when chronic anxiety takes hold of a family, it affects everyone and is even passed down from one generation to the next as the dysfunctional forms of handling chronic anxiety are modeled as the family norm. This generational dysfunctional adaptation to chronic anxiety typically takes the form of an uneasy balance of expectations between one or more individuals with "problems" and the others who focus on that person's problem to keep their mind off their own issues. Sometimes the person with the identified problem is referred to as the "designated patient" and the ones who wrap their lives around trying to help or rescue the designated patient from themselves are sometimes identified as "co-dependents." "Designated patients" and "co-dependents" need each other and will tend to act in ways to keep the dance going no matter how dysfunctional and destructive it is.

2. The teeter-totter

This chronic, self-correcting balance is the second marker of family dysfunction. One of the great insights of Family Systems Theory is that relationships tend to follow well-worn paths. For example, think of someone you know really well. You know this person and she or he knows you. You trust each other. You know what to expect of each other. You know what this person likes and doesn't like. Now imagine yourself at a huge mall looking for a birthday present to give to this person at a party that night. Walking down the center of the mall, you see all kinds of stores. Some of them look like they may have something you think your friend would like to receive from you. Other stores you wouldn't think about going into on this particular shopping trip. Why? Because you know there is little chance there would be something in these stores your friend would expect to get from you.

You could, if you wanted to, go into one of the stores that was less likely to have something your friend would like and buy something totally out of character, something totally unexpected to come from you. If you were to do that one of two things would be likely to happen at the party that night. One, your gift would be received as a terrific joke, something so unexpected and goofy coming from you that everyone would naturally assume it was meant to be funny; *or* you could end up confusing or even offending your friend by giving something too out of character for your relationship. A specific example of this might be giving a gift that might be interpreted as romantic or sexy to someone who thinks of you more like a brother or sister than a love interest.

What Family Systems suggests is that not just some, but *all* relationships involve these kinds of balance of expectations. As the old proverbs says, "Birds of a feather flock together." We like being around people who will let us be ourselves. We like knowing what to expect from the people close to us. We like to think that we can count on the people around us and that they can count on us.

Still, even with people you trust and feel comfortable with, there will sooner or later come a time when one or the other of you has needs or desires the other may not be able to meet or may not want to meet. Say, for example, that you and your friend have decided to spend an evening together. You announce that you want to go to a movie. Your friend wants to stay home and watch TV.

If yours is a healthy or functional relationship, each of you will feel free to choose whether or not you want to (*a*) go to a movie, (*b*) stay home and watch TV, (*c*) decide to each go your separate way, (*d*) forget about tonight and get together some other time, (*d*) go out to dinner instead, or (*f*) do something completely different. If yours is an unhealthy or dysfunctional relationship, one or both of you may feel *compelled* to do what the other wants for fear that if you do not, the relationship itself would be in danger of being irreparably damaged. If yours is an unhealthy or dysfunctional relationship, one or the other of you might try to manipulate, bully, or in some other way force the other to do what you want to do regardless of what they want to do. This manipulation might take the form of pouting, begging, arguing, hitting, threatening to leave and never come back, getting drunk, giving the "silent treatment," or some other behavior that has worked in the past to help you to get your own way.

The difference between a healthy and an unhealthy relationship — one that is functional and one that is dysfunctional — is that in a healthy relationship, the persons involved choose which needs and desires they are willing or able to meet and which ones they are unable or unwilling to meet. In a healthy relationship, you buy the birthday gift you know your friend would like because you *want to* not because you *have to*. In a healthy relationship, deciding to go to the movies or stay home is not hugely significant because you are confident that the relationship is stronger than one night's broken engagement. In healthy relationships, the responsibility for the balance, the give and take of the relationship, is shared. Each person is flexible. Each person can be helpful or needy, strong or weak, happy or sad, funny or serious, satisfied or dissatisfied just because they are and the other person in the relationship is not threatened by this or feeling the need to fix the other person or change the situation. In a healthy relationship, each person knows that if the other is not able to or chooses not to meet a certain need or desire at a particular moment, in time the temporary feelings of disappointment will fade and the relationship will continue to grow and thrive.

In an unhealthy relationship, though, the balance tends to be fixed and rigid. Stepping out of character in the least way makes everyone else very nervous — another word for anxious. In a healthy relationship each person accepts the fact that sometimes the other person will not meet certain expectations. In an unhealthy relationship, however, an unmet expectation feels like a loaded gun held right between your eyes. Every hint of disappointment or disapproval in an unhealthy relationship is seen as a full-blown crisis threatening the very fabric of the relationship. In a healthy relationship, it is the *person* who counts. In an unhealthy relationship, the person tends to get lost as keeping the balance — the teeter-totter of expectations — is what really counts.

You see this sort of thing in someone who seems to get into one relationship after another and always with the "wrong" kind of person. If you were to examine the whole string of relationships, you would see that even though they involve different men or women and different circumstances, each of the relationships had the same manipulative, painful, dysfunctional "feel" to it. The classic example of this is the person who marries one alcoholic after another always insisting that this time it is going to be different.

In healthy relationships, each person is a total person. In dysfunctional/unhealthy relationships, people tend to become one or two dimensional cutout paper dolls. In a healthy relationship each person is allowed to have strengths and weaknesses; in unhealthy relationships, strengths and weaknesses are assigned and God help you if you pretend to be strong about something you are supposed to be weak about or weak about something you are supposed to be strong about. In a healthy relationship, the balance is allowed to go back and forth, up and down in a fun, playful way like a well-balanced teeter-totter. Each person is free to play or not play as they wish. Neither person feels himself or herself totally responsible for all the good things or all the problems in the relationship. Blame and credit for the good and the bad are shared. In an unhealthy relationship, the teeter-totter is rigged and going up and down or back and forth requires great effort and feels scary and painful. Neither partner is having fun, but neither can they stop for the dysfunctional rules of their relationship are what are driving them and not their own free wills.

In a healthy relationship, neither person feels herself at the mercy or control of the other. In a healthy relationship, the "dance" is voluntary and fun, not strained or constricting. Each person can take the lead. Each person is free to set-out a tune if he feels like it.

In an unhealthy, dysfunctional relationship, the balance is never even. There is little sense of back and forth, give and take. In a dysfunctional relationship, good guys are always good guys, and bad guys are always bad guys; heroes are always heroes and goats are always goats; victims are always victimized and rescuers are always rescuing. Unhealthy, dysfunctional relationships feel like a scene in an Old western movie where the bad guy shoots his gun at the feet of the good guy who has to "dance" to keep from getting his foot blown off. Or, as one counseling client I had described the unhealthy relationship she was in, it is as if the two have forgotten how to love each other and instead have become content with holding "mutual prisoners."

3. May I have the Oscar, please?

When a relationship is unhealthy or dysfunctional, the relationship balance becomes skewed or tilted toward one side or the other. Persons are allowed to have needs or to be helpful, but never both. The dance becomes mandatory with the steps predetermined and the choices of whether to dance, with whom, and for how long limited. Persons are not allowed to have both strengths and weaknesses. Instead of being three dimensional, fully functioning individuals, the people in dysfunctional relationships tend to become stuck in *roles* — the third mark of dysfunction.

A role is just what it sounds like — an act the individual plays to the exclusion of other personality traits. For example, say that somewhere along the way you got the message, "You are a leader." Ideally, that message helps you build a healthy self-esteem. You picture yourself as someone others trust and admire and then, if you choose, you can go out and actually become that person. With the image of yourself as a leader firmly in mind, your self-confidence and your example could inspire others to follow you.

But, if the message, "You are a leader," becomes unhealthy, then "You are a leader," gets turned into "You *must* be a leader at all times regardless of the circumstances, your competence, or your needs and if you ever fail to be a leader you will never be loved again." Instead of building a healthy self-esteem and enhancing your experience of life, the message now be-comes a sword hung over your head controlling your life and robbing you of choices. Instead of inspiring people with your ample gifts and abilities, chances are you become a bully who has to get your own way . . . or else! Your slogan becomes, "you must follow me," rather than, "I invite you to follow me." Challenges to your leadership may feel like threats to your very being. The joy of leading may instead feel like a millstone around your neck: heavy and onerous, but something you absolutely must bear.

Shakespeare once wrote, "All the world's a stage, and all the men and women merely players upon it." We all play the parts of "father," "sister," "employee," "friend," "child," "citizen" and the like. To the degree that we are aware of our actor status and can choose when, where, and how to perform, this is not a problem. But, when roles become straightjackets that dominate all aspects of our life, they can actually take over and steal life from us. This is what happens to those of us controlled by our experiences of family dysfunction. If you have ever felt that you couldn't take off the greasepaint and just be a regular person with certain family members or in certain circumstances, you know what I'm talking about. You have been caught up in a role without even knowing it.

Dysfunction at the Time of Death and Dying

Death and dying are about the most anxiety-producing experiences a per-son or a family can possibly go through. *Everyone* feels inadequate when it comes to knowing how to handle their own death or the death of some-one they love. If then, you are already chronically anxious *before* you have the added stress of death and dying, you can see how a time of death and dying is likely to be the proverbial straw that sends the camel to the orthopedic hospital.

Since almost all of us are chronically anxious and dysfunctional to some degree or other, almost every one of us falls back on the anxiety-coping mechanisms we learn in early childhood when faced with death, dying, and grief. If those mechanisms are less than healthy — and chances are that they are — death and dying will likely make the situation worse rather than better. We will attempt to manage our *anxiety* by playing the *roles* that have always worked to keep the *balance* of neediness and helpfulness, weakness and strength, function and dysfunction in our relationships in the past, hoping they will now help us deal with the difficult emotions brought on by death and dying. Or, to put it in other words, *when faced with an ultimate threat to the relationship we have always known and counted on, our tendency is to cease to be persons and to become characters in a family drama where each person says and does what we think the others expect us to say and do. None of us, therefore, have to actually face and admit to the new and uncomfortable feelings of fear and dread that we worry will overwhelm us and the family system.*

Or to put it as simply as I can: *death and dying tends to make the most capable and functional of us dysfunctional.* And when we become dysfunctional in the face of death and dying, we lose our ability to make it a time of healing. Jesus once quoted an old Jewish proverb, "Physician, heal thyself." The truth of this proverb is that no one is able to be a healing presence for someone else when they themselves are an emotional and spiritual mess. No one can create a healing environment for themselves or someone else while caught up in a role.

Roles and Death and Dying

Family System Theory describes four classical dysfunctional roles. My experience is that these four are indeed the typical roles that tend to be played out at the time of death and dying. Often these roles already exist in the family structure. You may have been aware of them all along. Or it is possible that the added stress of death and dying may heighten them beyond their normal "sub-clinical" levels so that you now see them for the first time.

Anyone involved in the experience — family members, friends, or even paid caregivers — can get caught up in playing one of these roles. Even the person who is dying may have one. Each of the roles is an attempt to control the anxiety of the situation by playing a predictable "part" in the relationship with the others — to be a "character" in the play if you will.

The role players do this unconsciously hoping that they and the family will thus be able to maintain a sense of emotional balance without having to deal with the real emotions of fear, anger, confusion, dismay, and worry that death and dying generate and that threaten to overwhelm them. It is an attempt to pretend that a situation that is totally out of control is under control by doing what has always worked in the past to keep uncontrollable situations masked and thus manageable.

Each of the roles comes with rules of behavior and each relates to the other roles in predictable ways. Here are the big four:

1. *The Hero:* The Hero, also known as "The-Super-Responsible-One," believes that he or she is the only one who can keep the family going regardless of ability, skill, time, personal sacrifice, or damage done to self or others. This role stereotypically falls to an eldest child. However, it is often gender-defined with some families putting these unrealistic expectations on the boys while other families expect the girls to pick them up whether they are the oldest or not.

The rules for the Hero read something like this: You must *always* appear to know what to do and when to do it. You are not allowed to show weakness. You are not allowed to admit to being tired. You are never to ask for help and may accept help only when it becomes clear you are totally exhausted or too incapacitated to continue to play the part. As the Hero you not only expect others to mess things up sooner or later, but you *count on it* to maintain your control. You must complain only when such complaining has the likelihood of generating feelings of guilt or shame in one or more of the others but will not actually bring about relief or structural change to make the situation better. The Hero's responsibility toward the other roles is one of supervisor or commanding general. Should the Hero drop from exhaustion — or if the Hero is the person who is dying — and is no longer able to function, the whole family will likely put pressure on someone else to take up this role out of fear that, without a Hero to tell them what to do and how to feel, anxiety will surely spiral out of control.

2. *The Pleaser:* The role of the Pleaser is to keep everyone as happy as possible for as long as possible no matter what the cost to self, others,

or authentic relationships. This person might also be thought of as the False Peacemaker or the Caretaker. The Pleaser must always appear to be compliant with the wishes of others, especially the Hero. The Pleaser should always avoid being responsible for making decisions, but should always be ready to jump to carry out the decisions of others, especially those of the Hero.

The Pleaser can take one of two forms or can alternate between the forms. The first form is that of the laid-back handler of any and all problems. This "no worries" attitude belies the sense of panic that lies just under the surface. The Pleaser choosing this form plays the part of the proverbial duck that is calm above the water while paddling frantically beneath the surface in an attempt to keep everything on an even keel. This placid veneer may provoke admiration in others who ask, "How can you be so relaxed with all this going on?" This praise is heady stuff for the Pleaser, who will be motivated to be even more pleasing.

The other form of the Pleaser is the classic "Nervous Nelly" who flits around taking care of everything and everyone all the time. Nervous Nelly (or Nervous Ned) is exhausting just to watch. This is the Martha role of the Mary and Martha story in the Bible. Though "just trying to be helpful," this form of the Pleaser is actually quite manipulative as the Pleaser goes around taking care of what others are perfectly able to take care of themselves. The Pleaser's constant attention to the needs of others eventually becomes so annoying people just want them to "sit down already!"

The Pleaser would never think of complaining.

3. *The Rebel* — Though the Rebel doesn't want to be boxed into a role, the very compulsion to be defiant keeps the Rebel a character caught up in the family drama. The Rebel role is to provide a lightning rod toward which everyone else can direct angry, negative feelings.

The Rebel role can also take two forms. One form of this role is to stay away and dare to have a fun, apparently carefree life while others labor with the stress of death and dying. If this form of rebellion is chosen, the others can avoid reality by gossiping and pouring on contempt from afar. The other form is to be constantly and annoyingly underfoot just daring the others to criticize and find fault. This is the path of picking fights whenever possible.

The Rebel form of dysfunction provides relief from the reality of death and dying by being so annoying that no one has time to think about death or dying. The Rebel will draw comments such as, "Why does she act that way?" or "Why doesn't he help out?" The Rebel is often seen as being selfish or self-absorbed. The Rebel often does nothing but complain.

As long as the Rebel is rebelling, the Hero can feel justified for feeling put upon for having to be in charge all the time. As long as the Rebel is rebelling, the Pleaser can keep on pleasing so that everyone will "just get along." The antics of the Rebel provide a smoke screen for the others to focus on so that they don't have to deal with (a) their feelings, (b) the fact that someone is dying, (c) their own sense of inadequacy, fear, and anxiety.

4. *The Lost Child:* The Lost Child is clueless, useless, always messing things up, out of it, confused, a basket case. The Lost Child may have spent a lifetime not succeeding or may take the occasion of death and dying to become incompetent. The Lost Child can never be counted on. The Lost Child always lets others down. The Lost Child may be the one with the active drug, alcohol, gambling, eating, or other addiction or compulsive disorder — provided the Rebel hasn't already claimed one or more of these. The Lost Child drifts aimlessly from one thing to anther without a sense of focus or purpose, never assuming responsibility and never cleaning up messes. The Lost Child doesn't complain. The Lost Child is the reason others complain.

As with the Rebel, the Lost Child provides for the Hero a reason to believe she can never relax even for a minute and for the Pleaser someone to smother with attention. An example of the Lost Child is the way Kevin's family treats him at the beginning of the movie *Home Alone.* As in *Home Alone,* the Lost Child is seldom as incompetent as the others make out, but the Lost Child's bumbling gives the family something to focus on and complain about rather than handle reality. A skillfully slothful Lost Child can make even a Rebel look good.

◆ ◆ ◆

As I mentioned above, some people seem to thrive on stress. They find stress invigorating and energizing. Stress seems to bring the best out in them. In the same way, some of the roles we assume to mask stress, anxiety, and dysfunction are sometimes seen by others as admirable. The Hero, for example, may get rave reviews for being a "take charge" person. The Pleaser might be thought of as a godsend by those who benefit from the countless hours spent taking care of others. The Rebel might conceivably be admired in some circles for demonstrating such a sense of independence.

But just because a role is praised doesn't make it any less of a role. A Hero might be indeed heroic, but she may also be using her heroic role to mask her true emotions and to create distance between herself and others. The Pleaser may derive great satisfaction from serving others, but his actions may also be a way of reinforcing dysfunctional family patterns.

If you are thinking, "I'm not playing a role; I'm doing this because I *like* to help out," try this simple test: stop doing what you are doing. If tension — your own or those of others — starts to spin out of control, if you start to get an overwhelming sense of guilt that you are letting the others down, or if there are not so subtle hints that "no one can do it the way you can": you are stuck in a role. Just because a workaholic is admired for being a millionaire by the time she is thirty doesn't negate the trail of damage she has done to herself, others, and her relationships in the pursuit of her goal. Just because a man is admired for always knowing what to do, that doesn't mean that his taking care of them is healthy for him or for the others. Just because you are spending countless hours by the side of your dying loved one doesn't mean that you are not using this act of devotion to mask feelings of resentment toward other family members or a sense of anxiety that if you don't do it, no one else will. I am not condemning being successful or helpful or attentive. I celebrate success. I give thanks for people who are helpful and willing to sacrifice on behalf of others. I am just trying to point out that dysfunction can sometimes look good, perhaps too good to be true.

Becoming Ourselves

Do any of these roles or situations feel familiar? If, as you read these descriptions you found yourself identifying with one or more — yes, it is possible to play more than one role — *congratulations!* You've just taken the first step in breaking out of your roles.

If a family is to come together to find healing when cure is no longer possible, the first thing it must do is acknowledge that it is caught up in role playing. It then has to begin the hard work of breaking out of the roles that have kept family members locked into their predictable patterns and prevented them from becoming full-fledged persons on their own. Family members have to become aware of their individual neediness and their individual abilities. They have to admit to their own weaknesses and claim their own strengths. They have to have the courage to feel the feelings they'd rather keep locked away.

The psychological term for becoming a fully functioning individual person is "differentiation." To differentiate is to become a complete person; to give up the role — be it positive or negative — that was assumed as a child and take responsibility for handing one's own anxiety. To differentiate is to be an "I" when the people around us are screaming "we" or "you." It is to be able to say, "I think [feel, believe] this," even if it is not what others want to hear. It is the ability to chart your own course when "we" are piling on the pressure to think, feel, believe or do what "we" say *ought* to be thought, felt, believed, or done. It is not knuckling under when challenged with "How can you think [say, believe, do] that?" It is to be able to offer help as you feel able to help or to ask for help when you need to ask for help. It is to be able not to help if you decide you can't or don't want to help or to refuse help if you don't believe you need help. It is to be "me" just as I am, right here, right now, with all my abilities and liabilities, strengths and weaknesses. It is to be a person, not a role, not a stereotype, not a memory, and not an expectation.

By this point, some of you reading this are starting to get excited. You are starting to believe that hope is on the way, that you can be freed from the roles that have limited and controlled you for as long as you can remember. You might have thought up till now that your longing to be a real, three-dimensional person is just a fantasy. I remember one person I worked with for months who knew in her soul that she was meant to be different from the expectations her family had placed on her, but who just couldn't allow herself to do the things that would enable her to put that dream into action. It was only over the course of several months and many anguished hours of self-reflection that she was finally able to break away and find her true self while at the same time staying connected to her family in a loving and appropriate way.

Others who are reading these words may feel yourselves starting to break out into a cold sweat, worried that if you were to try to put any of this into action and actually attempt to break out of your roles, your family would never forgive you. You don't really believe that self-differentiation is possible or that if it is possible, it is something you could ever achieve yourself.

Both of these reactions are perfectly understandable. If your family is like most families, roles have been assigned and the teeter-totter has been unevenly loaded for as long as anyone can remember. To try to suddenly break out of the roles now will most likely be seen by other family members as (*a*) unloving, (*b*) ungrateful, (*c*) dangerous, (*d*) crazy, or (*e*) all the above. What did you expect? Remember, what you are trying to do is break out of the roles of relating to one another that have been standard operating procedure for years and maybe generations. Just because *you* want to be real doesn't mean the others do. You are introducing a change into the family system. *Of course* the others are going to wonder what you are dong and may even — either overtly or covertly — try to get you to change back to the way you were before.

Self-Differentiation

So then, how do you break out of roles? You have already started. To simply acknowledge that you are caught up in playing a role is to gain power over it. Much like the character "Neo" in the movie *The Matrix*, your eyes have been opened and you can see the world as it really is. You can now begin to watch yourself in action. With practice you will soon be able to catch yourself when you are caught up in role playing. You will be able to identify those old "Gotcha!" feelings that accompany role-playing.

What are the "Gotcha!" feelings of being trapped in a role? Let's look at an example. Let's say that a big decision has to be made and you find yourself to be the one expected to make it. You could, if you were a healthy, three-dimensional person with strengths and weaknesses, abilities and liabilities, choose one of several options. You could: (*a*) consult with friends or professionals who know more about this situation than you do, (*b*) solicit ideas and opinions from friends or family members who have gone through something similar, (*c*) defer the decision to someone else who you feel has more wisdom about the situation than you do, (*d*) pray about it and wait for divine inspiration, (*e*) make the decision democratically by calling for a vote of relevant parties, (*f*) something I haven't thought of, or (*g*) some combination of all the above.

But, if you are caught up in the role of the Hero, you wouldn't think of letting someone else share your burden. As Hero, you would naturally assume that it is all up to you to make this decision and that the others either will not or cannot be of any help. Here is what you will most likely do. You will: (*a*) feel that this decision is yours and yours alone and that you cannot risk showing yourself incompetent by asking for help in making it, (*b*) berate yourself for being so stupid and for not being a better decision maker, (*c*) stress out, lose sleep, overeat, smoke too much, not be able to eat, drink too much, or some combination of all of the above, (*d*) feel angry toward other family members because once again they are expecting you to take care of this — just like you have to take care of everything else! (*e*) finally make the decision, (*f*) be on your guard lest someone challenge or criticize what you've decided — just like they always do, and (*g*) go through the same wicked circle the next time a decision is necessary.

If you are a role player, just reading this is likely to make your gut tighten as you feel the familiar trap of family dysfunction starting to spring — Gotcha!

I could have offered "Gotcha!" examples from any of the four classic roles. The Pleaser who tries to let someone else wait on him only to feel the anxiety build till he has to jump up and pitch in — Gotcha! The Lost Child who announces she is going to finally pull her own weight and help out only to find that the others have devised their own ways of doing things and the Lost Child is stuck hopelessly fouling things up . . . again — Gotcha! The Rebel who tries to reconcile with her family, but only ends up creating more hard feelings till the pressure builds up and she has to cut and run — Gotcha! You could probably describe many more examples from your particular role: times when you or someone else has tried to do something different, to meet a situation more honestly or more humanly, only to compulsively revert to tried and trusted patterns when the anxiety got too great. These dramas repeat themselves over and over again with thousands of variations on the themes.

There is another variation on role playing among people who are otherwise healthy and functional individuals. Role playing can be situational. For example, the person in my Hero illustration above might, in her day-to-day life, be a capable and skilled decision maker in her professional setting. She might be known as someone who seeks the opinions of others and who works to build strong coalitions. She might be able to make decisions involving life-and-death issues, large sums of money, or vast numbers of people and sleep like a baby at night. But when it comes to making a decision involving a close family member, it is a whole different matter. I remember a banker I once worked with. He was the head of a major division of his company with dozens of people reporting to him. But when his father got sick and was nearing death, he became a six-year-old playing once again the role of doing whatever it took to please his Daddy.

That's the power of roles. No matter how differentiated and healthy we may be in other aspects of our lives, roles keep us locked into ways of thinking, feeling, and acting that we learned as children when thrown into anxious family situations. Away from home we might be capable, individuated, responsible adults. Within the family circle, we revert to scared second graders trying to survive the unspoken tensions and coping in the only way we know how.

There is real power, then, in learning to be aware of when and how you get caught up in playing roles. Once you are aware of the roles you play and what triggers you to revert to role, you will be able to make deliberate decisions about whether you want to continue in that role or to change your behavior to something more honest and mature.

With time and careful self-observation, you will be able to identify the emotions and situations that trigger your dysfunctional roles. You will never be 100 percent free of roles or the emotions that trigger them. The goal is not to try to control the uncontrollable emotions, but to learn how to monitor and change the *behaviors* these emotions generate. Self-differentiated people have the same emotional responses to stress and anxiety as everyone else. The difference is that they have learned to intentionally and deliberately *respond* to those emotions and not just reflexively and unthinkingly *react* to them. By making an intentional response rather than a reflexive reaction, self-differentiated people have the ability to work through stressful situations to move toward health, wholeness, and healing and away from dysfunction and hurt.

Jesus once said, "You will know the truth, and the truth will set you free." Self-knowledge of the truth of when and how you get caught up in roles and understanding that you *can* break out of those roles if you want to is the first step in the long road to emotional and spiritual freedom.

Staying Yourself

Now that you are learning to be aware of the roles you play and what triggers those roles, the next step is not to let anyone force you back into the roles. In a sane, rational world, this would involve a simple heart-to-heart talk with the others members of your family. In a sane, rational world, your family would hear what you are saying and immediately recognize the wisdom of your words. They would agree, "Oh yes, we see now. Thank you for helping us to understand. From now on we're all going to stop playing roles and start being real with each other."

Unfortunately, we don't live in a sane, rational world. We live in a messy real world where the very emotional anxieties that cause us to fall into roles in the first place now work to try to keep us locked in them. By breaking out of your role, you will send a tsunami-sized ripple through your family structure that the others will more than likely do their best to resist. The anxiety your new behaviors generate will get them to do their best to get you to go back to your old ways so as to restore the balance and maintain the old painful teeter-totter ride. So, if you are going to suddenly break out of your old patterns, you'd better expect to meet some resistance. Self-differentiation is scary, often lonely work. If you are going to be an emotional pioneer venturing into this brave new world of emotional honesty, you are going to need some help. I have three suggestions.

First, find someone you can lean on to help you stay the course. I recommend joining an ACA (Adult Child of Alcoholics), Co-Dependent, or Al-anon group even if your family dysfunction does not involve alcohol. These self-help groups can be found all over the country. They are sometimes run by a therapist, but are most often associated with Alcoholics Anonymous. AA, in my opinion, does nothing short of work miracles as individuals reach out in honest love to help other individuals break out of destructive compulsive, dysfunctional patterns. To find an AA sponsored Co-dependent group, look in the phone book under AA. There is no charge to attend a meeting though they may ask for a small donation to cover the costs of coffee and the meeting room. The patterns of family dysfunction, dependency, and co-dependency are the same in all dysfunctional situations. At AA you will find people who know what you are going through and will support your decision to be an individual.

A second suggestion to help you as you begin to self-differentiate is to look to a friend who has worked successfully on self-differentiation and is willing to coach you along. In AA, this person is called a "sponsor." Sometimes, if you are lucky enough to be in an honest, supportive relationship, your spouse or significant other may be close enough to your family situation to give you insight into your roles and yet have enough distance to offer you clues as to what triggers those roles and when you are caught up in one. Be careful, though, when using your spouse or significant other as a coach. An attempt to point out dysfunctional patterns in your family of origin may be perceived as a personal attack and not a helpful suggestion.

My third suggestion is that, even after you have found a self-help group and you have recruited a friend, spouse, or other family member who is willing to coach you as you step out of your roles, you also find an outsider to work with. A counselor, psychologist, clinical social worker, chaplain, clergyperson, doctor, or other counseling professional who understands family dynamics and the ways death and dying turn up the heat on dysfunction will be a valuable ally in helping you build the "you" you want to be. You need someone you can turn to in order to help you hold on to your resolve not to revert to roles when the pressures to "change back" become too much for you to handle on your own. Even if you have to pay for these services, it will be money well spent.

Starting to Differentiate at the Time of Death and Dying

You have decided that you are going to find healing in death and dying. You are determined to break out of your tired, old roles and be a real person. You've built yourself a support system of friends and professionals. *Now* what do you do?

First, take a very deep breath. Then pray...a lot. Then jump in with both feet!

The place to start is to find a way to let your family know what you are up to. This may not be easy, especially if your family's dysfunctionalism is particularly violent. My best advice is to be as direct and nonjudgmental as you can be. Let them know that you love them very much and that you are not blaming anyone. Do your best to explain what you are trying to do and why you are trying to do it. Try to show how stepping out of roles and facing death and dying honestly, openly, and courageously will help *them,* too. Tell them as clearly and firmly as you can that you are not going to play roles any more. Tell them that this time of death and dying is too important to waste stuck in tired old patterns of relating that have never really worked before and aren't going to work this time, either. Invite them to join you in your resolve to face the reality of death in as real a way as you can. Invite them to your ACA, Co-dependent, or Al-anon meeting. Share this book with them. Take them to meet with your professional counselor.

You may be pleasantly surprised to find that some family members will be very receptive to what you are trying to do. If you have grown tired of family games and roles, it is entirely likely others have, too. At the very least, you owe it to yourself, and them, to try. If they do not wish to join you on your path to healing, that is their decision. At least they and you will be clear about what you will and will not be doing as the process of dying unfolds.

This takes us to what is perhaps the biggest stumbling block to breaking out of roles during the highly emotional and intensely personal time of death and dying. The months, weeks, and days surrounding death and dying tend to be filled with a crushing load of things that have to be done. Someone has to schedule and coordinate medical appointments and visiting medical personnel. Someone has to make sure that medications are given and taken at their proper times and in their proper doses. Someone has to make sure the bills are kept track of. Transportation to doctor appointments and visits to the hospital or other care facilities need to be arranged and provided. If you are planning to do home care, there are physical arrangements to be made: hospital supplies to order, special food to be prepared, routines to be shifted. Someone will need to schedule the people who will be helping out. Someone will need to keep everyone informed of what is happening. And all this has to happen *in addition to* all the normal responsibilities of running a household, taking care of children, and handling a job.

All this busyness and the physical and emotional exhaustion that follow tend to take us back to our old roles and games. The old roles and games are what we know best. They are comfortable, if not particularly functional or fulfilling. But when you are worn out with work and worry it is simply much easier to slip into one of your old patterns than to stay the course of a new way of relating to yourself and others. Handling death and all the fuss and fury that accompanies dying is enough to frazzle the most emotionally stable person! And since none of us comes from a better than 60 percent healthy background, who of us is strong enough to resist the temptation to slip into the tired old routines of roles we already know rather than trying to forge a whole new way of relating to one another?

What is needed is a way to separate the *tasks* that need to be done from the emotionally assigned *roles* that have always handled those tasks in the past. What is needed is a way to get things done while at the same time giving each person involved the emotional space and security to express and act on their real feelings without the pressure to conform to dysfunctional patterns. Or, to say it in another way, we need to find a way in the emotionally charged face of death and dying to remain *human beings* and not revert to *human doings*.

There are certain tasks or *functions* that need to be handled at the time of death and dying if the situation is to go smoothly and efficiently. Failure to provide for these functions will increase the pressure to revert to roles. Finding a creative way to handle the myriad tasks that accompany death and dying will help to create the healing environment you are working so hard to make.

Giving Up Roles and Taking Up Functions

Death and dying is a lot of work, particularly if you want to make it a time of healing. How, then, do you make sure things get done while at the same time avoiding those well-worn dysfunctional roles that have kept you prisoner for so long? The answer is to make a careful distinction between *roles* and *functions*.

As I've said above, *roles* are the manipulative ways we learned to avoid taking responsibility for our feelings and anxieties. *Functions*, on the other hand are "takin' care of business" in such a way that we remain whole, healthy, warm-blooded, three-dimensional human beings. Roles and functions can look a lot alike to the untrained eye. The difference is that roles are *unconsciously and permanently assigned* while functions are *intentionally and temporarily assumed*.

Roles are the unconscious part of the dysfunctional teeter-todder that we take up because of the unspoken assumptions and manipulations of the family system. Roles are the way dysfunctional families defend themselves against emotional tension and stress by forging repetitive, predictable patterns of behavior that bleed off the tension and stress, but at the expense of genuine intimacy and caring. Because they have been with us from childhood, roles tend to be rigid and attached to our very self-identity. They often lead to feelings of resentment and bitterness as they become more and more burdensome over time. Roles can be shed, but only with extreme effort, and often the very thought of shedding a role can be terrifying.

Functions, on the other hand, are tasks that are voluntarily and intentionally taken on as the need arises. Functions are stand-alone tasks that need to get done. Who will do them, when they get done, and how they are accomplished are matters open to negotiation. They are not attached to our personality structures. The individuals involved get to pick the functions they will perform and can freely trade with others as time, ability, and emotional wherewithal ebb and flow. The completion of functions is flexible. Taking on a function for a loved one in need is a gift of authentic love and not a duty or burden. Taking on a function may require some personal sacrifice, but it is one that is assumed willingly and not compulsively or resentfully.

People who get caught up in roles have little choice in the matter. People who have a function have a multitude of choices. For example, a person caught up in the Hero role may feel she *has* to keep everyone informed of the progress of the disease, the arrangements that have been made, when to visit, etc. whether he wants to or is able to or not. Further, she may feel she *must* continue to do this. However, the person who has taken up the function of Communications Center enjoys and *wants* to keep everyone informed and may at some point decide pass that function off to someone else for some period of time.

In a healing experience of death, the individuals involved give up their roles while making sure the functions still get done. What would this look like? It might look like a Hero who takes a regular "day off" and lets the Lost Child take charge for twenty-four hours. It may look like a Pleaser who lets the Rebel wait on her for a change.

There are *three rules*, though, that must be obeyed if this exchange of roles for functions is going to work. To violate these rules, either intentionally or unintentionally, is the surest way to sabotage the healthy system you are trying to create and plunge everyone back into dysfunction.

The first rule of stepping out of roles to take up a function is to *thoroughly and completely describe the task that must be done and when it must be accomplished*. This is not as easy as it may sound. It is easy to assume that the other person knows all about the particulars of a task when that is not the case. You may have been doing a particular task for so long that it is second nature. You don't even have to think about it anymore and it may not even cross your mind to explain the subtle nuances of the task you have learned over the years or what to do if a problem comes up. You may assume that because it is so easy for you to accomplish this particular task, *anyone* could do it just as effortlessly. If then, you are sincere about stepping outside your roles and sharing your burden with others, it is up to you to spell out as best you can the whats, whens, hows, and whys of each task or function to be accomplished.

An example is the simple task of driving a loved one to the medical center for treatments. Let's say that you have been performing this simple task for a long time. Someone else offers to take over for you and you accept. When she asks, "How much time does it take to get to the medical center from here?" you may honestly answer, "Half an hour." Much to your surprise, she may come back from the medical center frustrated and accusing you of lying to her because what you said was a thirty-minute trip took them over an hour, and they ended up missing the appointment. Thinking back on what happened, you realize you simply forgot to mention that since you had been making this trip for so long you had learned the traffic patterns at that time of day and had found a shortcut that made the trip much quicker and easier. So part of handing a task off to someone else is to share all you know about that task.

The second rule is this: *unless critical to the task itself, the way the task is accomplished is not as important as the fact that it is actually accomplished.* A well-worn manipulative technique that allows dysfunction to continue even though you may say you are trying to stop it is to allow someone else to assume a task you've always done and then criticize the way they do it until they get angry and quit. A classic example is the Pleaser who lets someone else use her kitchen to fix dinner, and then criticizes him for not putting all the pots and dishes back exactly as she had them. A variation on this is the Hero who lets someone else make a decision and then nitpicks and second-guesses. As our grandmothers taught us, "there is more than one way to skin a cat," or to make a bed, or to prepare a meal, or to go to the store, or to do almost anything. There is no hard and fast rule that you have to drive to the medical center along a particular route — though it is still considerate to pass on vital traffic information if you have it.

So if you are the normal doer of a certain task and you have a particular way you've worked out to accomplish it efficiently and effectively and that is the way you would like to have it done, it is up to *you* to share that insight with whoever is taking over the job. To withhold this insight and then find fault when things are not done exactly as you want is *your* fault, not theirs. Also, just because you share your insight is no guarantee that your advice will be followed.

The exception to this rule that the doer of the task gets to decide how the task gets done is when the way the task is done is critical to the task itself. I am thinking in particular of certain medical procedures that family members may be taught to perform in a homecare situation. If the nurse tells you to flush a line a particular way or to give medication at a specific time, *everybody* needs to do this in the exact same way. No exceptions. It is up to the person who is trained to make sure that everyone knows this particular task is not a "dealer's choice" situation. This brings us to our third rule.

The third rule is simply this: *no complaining.* Be thankful the job got done and that you didn't have to do it. It may have taken longer than it would have taken you to do it. It may not look like, or taste like, or come out as it would have if you had done it yourself. But so what? The task was accomplished and the burden was shared. Real emotions were felt and shared and not camouflaged behind a role. Someone else had an opportunity to give a gift of love, time, and attention. And this is *much* more important than some tired old notion that it has got to be done my way.

Blessed are the flexible, for they shall not be bent out of shape.

Functions at the Time of Death and Dying

Every situation is unique, but these are the functions I have found to be most important at the time of death and dying:

1. Communications Center: The process of death and dying involves a lot of people all doing various, important tasks. Medical personnel, care providers, and supply venders need to be scheduled. Last minute changes have to be accommodated. Friends and family want to know the latest medical news. Friends call and want to know the best time to drop by. Meanwhile, all the "stuff" of life — getting the kids to school and activities, going to the store, handling a job, etc. — still have to be taken care of. Trying to coordinate all that coming and going requires clear, reliable communication. You need a Communications Center. The Communications Center is to be the official call-in point. It is the number family, friends, and professionals can contact to find out the real story. It is the place where messages can be left and reliably passed on to the proper person in a timely manner. The Communications Center helps everyone feel more comfortable by knowing the information they have is accurate and that they are fully "in the know."

Handling the Communications Center is a big job, but modern technology can help simplify the task. Some families make the official contact number a cell phone. That way, the phone can be passed on to someone else if the first Communications Center person needs to step down for a while. Email is another effective tool for communicating to a large number of people all at once. A weekly note can be sent out to a whole list of persons with the latest developments and updates on decisions and conditions. A notebook in which all incoming and outgoing phone calls are dated and notes on conversations recorded is one way to keep track of appointments and contacts. A bulletin board or a designated message center in the hall or on the refrigerator door that everybody knows to check is a way of making sure messages are passed on. Use your imagination to make things as simple and efficient as much as possible.

2. Decision Maker. There are routine, everyday "minor decisions" to be made. And there are "major decisions" to be made. Above I listed four legal tools to help you with the major decisions — the Living Will, the Durable Power of Attorney, the Durable Power of Attorney for Health Care, and a Last Will and Testament (see pages 61–64). The decision about who will make these major decisions needs to be made early in the dying process. Also, everyone involved with the death needs to know who carries these responsibilities. As I've emphasized above, the primary concern is to respect and carry out both the letter and the spirit of the wishes of the person who is dying. Seeing to this is the primary responsibility of the one who makes the major decisions.

In addition to the major decisions, there are dozens of minor decisions that need to be made. These everyday decisions — what to have for dinner, what movie to rent, when should the home health aide come by — can almost always be shared. By sharing decision making, you can keep everyone feeling like they are contributing in a positive way and relieve some of the burden from the major decision maker.

3. Entertainment/Comic Relief: I'll say it again. Dealing with death, dying, and grief are hard emotional and spiritual work. Everyone helping with the situation is going to need a break from time to time. The function of Entertainment/Comic Relief is to keep the situation from getting too grim. This function is also fairly easy to pass around. Take turns planning the weekend field trip. Make meals and even minor holidays and family get-togethers into important occasions. Have a dress-up night. Celebrate Christmas in June or Halloween in April. Children are naturals to help with this one.

4. Peacemaker: Dealing with death and dying can make even the most saintly of us "lose it" from time to time. In spite of the most competent Communications Center, messages will get lost and schedules can get fouled up. When tensions are high, tempers can flare. Things can be said that aren't meant to be said. Small voice inflections or looks can be interpreted as having far more significance than ever intended. Things can be heard that were never meant to be understood in the way they were. The function of Peacemaker is to keep a human face on everyone. It is to be a reminder that forgiving and being forgiven are truly divine. Peacemaking reminds everyone to stop, take a deep breath, count to 10 (or 100!), and try it again. The Peacemaker is the referee who keeps the game moving in spite of occasional rules infractions or steps out of bounds. Because Peacemaking can be a high-pressure position, it is particularly important to keep this function moving around so no one person gets burned out. Also, persons with Pleaser tendencies need to be careful that this function doesn't push all their role buttons.

5. Transportation Hub: There is often a lot of running around in death and dying. Doctor appointments need to be kept. Trips to the hospital or nursing home have to be coordinated. Prescriptions and equipment need to be picked up. Dozens of errands and last-minute trips to the store come up. The Transportation Hub doesn't necessarily have to do all the running, it but makes sure that the running gets taken care of.

6. Other: I encourage you to have your eyes open for any other function that may come up, particularly if you see a task becoming a pathway for falling back into roles. Some of these other functions may be long term. For example, a family where English is not the primary language may need to create the function of Translator. Some functions may be short-term or maybe one-time only. For example, you may need the one-time services of a Handyman who can install a riser on the seat of the toilet or handrails in the bathtub.

Keeping the Functions Sorted Out

Keeping track of functions is not easy, especially since they may look very much like roles, which you want to avoid. Expect to make mistakes. Expect that the ball will be dropped from time to time. And, when mistakes happen and the ball is rolling away from you and heading out the door, there will be a strong urge to revert to roles. The Hero will just *know* in his bones that none of this would have happened if he had been in charge and will be on the lookout for a way to take over once again. The Lost Child will inevitably expect herself to goof something up and, when she does, she will feel helpless to fix things and look for someone to bail her out. The Pleaser will feel her blood pressure rise as unhappiness raises its ugly head and will want to step in and "make everything better." The Rebel will feel the urge to make his escape to places unknown as the load of responsibility and expectation starts to bear down.

Tempers may flare. Unkind things may be said. Doors may be slammed. Blame may be thrown around by the bucketful. The Peacemaker may find herself in over her head trying to sort things out.

This is when you need to steel your resolve. Repeat to yourself, "I will *not* revert to role! I will *not* revert to role!" Keep your eye on the goal: a healing experience of death where people are real with one another through all the anxieties and pressures to revert to being puppets pulled about by strings.

As tensions rise and pressures to give up your quest for healthy relationships mount, it will seem like the most natural thing in the world to abandon your attempts to do a new thing. It will seem that this new way of relating to one another is just too hard, not worth the effort involved. When this happens, remember why you started down this path in the first place: your old dysfunctional ways of relating have not served you or your loved ones well. Your old family dynamics have forced you into a role that has become a burden keeping you from the intimacy you crave.

I have four ideas on how you might keep yourself from falling back into a role when the pressure of completing all the tasks and fulfilling all the functions of dealing with death and dying mount.

First, get everyone together as early as possible in the death and dying process. Sit down together *before* the pressures get unbearable and talk about each of the functions and discuss how you are going to handle them in your particular situation. Take them one function at a time. Ask, for example, "What kinds of communication needs are likely to arise in our situation? What resources do we have and what technology do we need to invest in?"

Go down the list. Talk about both major decisions and minor decisions and how you are going to handle them. Ask who might be the natural Peacemaker and who can serve as back up. Make some decisions about Entertainment/Comic Relief. You might want to start a list of activities everyone enjoys. Consider what transportation needs might arise. List as many one-time or long-term special needs as you can think of.

Work together until you have a plan for how you are going to handle things before they come up. Some families make a chart or mark a calendar matching functions with people and dates or even times of day. It may make sense to have a daytime Communications Center and an evening Communications Center. You might find it helpful to have a weekday Transportation Hub and a weekend Transportation Hub. I know one family where five of the six adult children and their families lived close by and one was a few hours away. They worked out a schedule for spelling each other on a rotating basis with the family from out of town coming up every weekend or two to give the local folks a rest. Consider what written instructions need to be drawn up and where to post them. You might want to put together a master notebook with phone numbers, what-to-do's, instructions, procedures, etc. and put it in a prominent place where *everybody* knows where it is and can contribute to it as need arises. If critical medical procedures or times for medications are known, make sure whoever is on duty knows how to do what needs to be done and who to call if they have a problem.

In short, try to work out as many details as you can think of as early in the process as possible. Write your plan down. Review, refine, renegotiate, and reassign as necessary.

Second, expect to make mistakes. No plan is foolproof. Unexpected complications will always come up. Resources you counted on will not materialize. Some people may become too tired and need to rest for a while. Some who said they would help may not be able to help and others who thought they would not be available may be able to clear their calendars. Anticipate mistakes and complications and talk together about what you are going to do about them. Make several plan "B's" and "C's" and maybe even a few "D's." Draw up a list of resources and people you may be able to call upon if things start falling apart. If you are in a hospice or other assisted program, see if there is social worker who can direct you to external resources you had never thought of.

Third, give yourselves permission to be human. One of the marks of people caught up in roles is that they take themselves *very* seriously. If you feel yourself reverting to a role, have the grace and good common sense to have a good laugh at yourself. So you messed up. So you blew your top. So you let someone down. So something did not go according to plan. So you broke out into a stark raving Hero or your Pleaser came roaring out and splashed all over everyone. So you took off and hid as a Rebel or your Lost Child emerged and you felt bewildered and had to ask for help. *So what?* In the words of Scarlett O'Hara, "Tomorrow is another day." You all have been practicing your roles for years. You are good at them. What makes you think you can break out of them in just a few weeks? You are only human. You are allowed to be less than perfect. You are allowed to make mistakes, and you are capable of fixing them when they happen.

And finally, when you slip up and revert to roles again — and you will — use those outside helpers you identified early in the process. Go to an ACA or Al-Anon meeting. Call on your spouse, friend, therapist, spiritual advisor, doctor: whoever you identified as someone who could help you break out of your roles. Make your confession of sin: you went back to roles. Accept their forgiveness and take their advice on getting back on course. If you picked the right persons, they will not only be expecting your call, they will be delighted to be of help. No one can completely remake their way of relating without help. Every new venture needs a little "course correction" from time to time. Call a brief "time out" and then get back into the game as soon as you are ready. Use your outside helpers. That is what they are there for.

Chapter Nine

Facing the Impossible

Issues Raised in Chapter Eight

Everything I've written so far is a lot easier for me to say than it is for you to do. I know. I've already made almost any mistake you can imagine.

A wise friend of mine once commented, "Conflict is inevitable, but combat is optional." It is possible for stress and tension to cause us to be at odds with someone without our going to the next level of threats and blame and roles. You can experience your feelings of loss, anger, loneliness, and worry without having to pretend they aren't affecting you and without taking them out on someone else. You do not have to continue to be trapped in roles just because you always have been.

Your Family Can do This

I have lifted up the issue of family dysfunction and how death and dying makes even the most loving and caring family tend to revert to roles they learned years ago. The following questions will help you reflect on the roles you play and what you can do to be more real.

- What stresses, conflicts, pressures, or chronic anxieties have you had to deal with over the years?

- What evidence (symptoms) of chronic anxiety can you identify in your life?

  - Overeating

  - Alcohol or drug abuse

  - Compulsive shopping

  - Complaining, nagging, or controlling others

  - Excessive caretaking or worrying

  - Compulsive use of sex or pornography

  - Smoking

  - Undereating or excessive weight loss

  - Other compulsive behavior

  - Creating emotional or physical distance

  - Being "clueless"

  - Other symptoms

- Have you ever been praised for acting out a role or stereotype others found admirable?

- Have you ever been criticized for acting out a role or stereotype others found annoying?

- Have you ever felt the pressure to fill a certain role or stereotype?

- How do you use one or more of these "drugs" to make you feel better when you can't take it any more?

  - Alcohol

  - Street drugs (which ones?)

  - Prescription medications

  - Shopping

- Internet browsing

- Pornography

- Tobacco

- Food

- Sex

- Nagging, fighting, or fault finding

- Working out

- Spending extra time at the job

- Watching TV

- Hobbies or pastimes

- Sleeping

- Avoiding others

- Other

- Have you found that you need higher or more frequent doses of your "drug" in order to get the same relief?

- What other things do you do to try to control the world around you?

- What kind of "teeter-totter" have you had to balance to handle the expectations that have been placed on you?

- Who have been stuck on the teeter-totter with you?

- Who do you feel you can be your real self around?

- Who do you feel you still can't be your real self around?

- Think of the relationships you are in right now. Which ones feel fixed and rigid?

- Which ones feel flexible and free?

- Which of the classic roles best describes you:

  - The Hero

  - The Pleaser

- – The Rebel
- – The Lost Child
- – Other

- ◆ Which of your behaviors let you know you are caught up in a role?
- ◆ Which of your behaviors would you like to change?
- ◆ What is most exciting about the idea of breaking out of your roles?
- ◆ What is most terrifying about the idea of breaking out of your roles?
- ◆ Where does the nearest ACA or Al-Anon group meet?

  - – When do they meet?
  - – How often are you attending?

- ◆ Who can help you break out of your roles?
- ◆ Do you have the name of a good therapist who can help you? How would you find one?
- ◆ Which specific tasks might go under each of these functions?

  - – Communications Center
  - – Decision Maker
  - – Entertainment/Comic Relief
  - – Peacemaker
  - – Transportation Hub
  - – Other short-term tasks
  - – Other long-term tasks

- ◆ Who could most easily assume each of these functions?

  - – Communications Center
  - – Decision Maker
  - – Entertainment/Comic Relief
  - – Peacemaker

- – Transportation Hub
- – Other short-term tasks
- – Other long-term tasks

◆ Who could serve most easily as backup for each of these functions?

- – Communications Center
- – Decision Maker
- – Entertainment/Comic Relief
- – Peacemaker
- – Transportation Hub
- – Other short-term tasks
- – Other long-term tasks

◆ What plan "B's" have you come up with for each of these functions?

- – Communications Center
- – Decision Maker
- – Entertainment/Comic Relief
- – Peacemaker
- – Transportation Hub
- – Other short-term tasks
- – Others long-term tasks

◆ What are you going to do when your best laid plans fail?

◆ Have you taken time to laugh at yourself today?

Issues Not Mentioned Anywhere Else

There are always things that come up that don't fit into a particular category. Here are some other issues that might arise as you deal with the death and dying of a loved one. You can also list here people you can call on when you feel the waters starting to get too deep.

- Who can help you house, feed, and transport out-of-town family friends who will be coming for the funeral?

- What might you do with clothing and personal effects that are not wanted by family and friends?

- What do you need to be doing to prepare survivors or children for what happens next?

- What cultural or ethnic traditions or expectations need to be considered?

- Who could help you with these?

- Who can help you handle with the legal and insurance issues that need to be taken care of?

Caregivers need to build a support network for themselves to hold off burnout.

- List the names and phone numbers of people you can call on when you need a break.

- List the names and phone numbers of people you can call on to help with transportation.

- List the names and phone numbers of people who can sit with the person who is dying awhile so you can get out of the house.

- List some specific tasks and the names and phone numbers of people who might help you with them:

Do not let my lack of imagination restrict your thinking. The questions above just scratch the surface. Take some time to consider what you might need to add to my list to meet your particular needs and circumstances. Fill a pad of paper with your own questions and answers. Get the others involved. Go back over your lists every few days and make changes and updates as necessary.

Appendix A

Planning a Funeral
or Memorial Service

From time immemorial, human beings have paused to remember and honor their dead with rites and rituals. Cave drawings and archeological digs have found evidence of funeral and memorial ceremonies going back to the dawn of human civilization. Early scientists in ancient Egypt and South America applied their knowledge of herbs and minerals to the embalming of human remains in some of the world's first examples of applied technology. The pyramids of Egypt and Central America, many of the great chapels of Europe, the Taj Mahal in India, and many of the world's greatest paintings, sculptures, and works of music were created to memorialize a departed loved one. Almost every town in the United States has at least one cemetery with markers made of stone intended to serve as lasting reminders of the lives of the people who are buried there.

Why do we go to all this trouble to surround death with solemn ceremony and expensive memorials? Paleontologists might suggest the rituals were a way for primitive cultures to attempt to control death. Historians might describe the pomp and circumstance surrounding the burial of a great political leader as a way for a society to assure itself that the important marks of its cultural identity will go on uninterrupted. Psychologists may point to the elaborate graves and memorials of the wealthy as attempts to provide for their own immortality. Religious people have always understood funerals and memorials as a way of reaffirming their faith in God as those they love move from one form of life to another. Families and friends gather at the graveside as a way to say good-bye to their loved ones and to reaffirm their bonds of love, to announce to the world that the circle will *not* be broken.

People today are not so different from people of the past. We draw strength and comfort from funerals and memorials for much the same reasons they did. I would like to suggest that modern funerals or memorial services offer three very specific benefits to those who are left behind after the death of a loved one. First, they are a way to mark the passing of a life. They note that this person was born and made a difference in the lives of others. Further, a funeral or memorial is a way to celebrate a person's accomplishments and legacy. It may also be an opportunity for the deceased to leave a final word of blessing to those left behind.

Second, funerals and memorials are an opportunity for loved ones, friends, and the community to say good-bye. They are an opportunity for friends and family to talk about the significance of the individual and to face the reality of death.

Finally, funerals and memorials are a chance for family and friends to share their grief and to be comforted by their continuing bonds with one another. It is an opportunity to share tears and laughter. It is a time to affirm that death is a part of life and that life continues after death.

Why Bother to Have a Service?

There was a time when no one would have thought of *not* having a funeral or memorial service. Today, I hear people asking if it is worth the bother and expense and some even saying they don't want any kind of a service at all. Some of the reasons for not having a service make sense. Services can be expensive. They are emotional. They can often feel hollow or hypocritical, especially for a family whose members are estranged from one another. I remember one funeral I performed where three people showed up. Before the afternoon was over, each of them had confided in me how much they hated each other and the deceased and that they had come to the funeral only out of a sense of obligation.

Some reasons for not having a service do not make sense; at least they don't make sense to me. Some people want to avoid a funeral or memorial because they don't feel they ever did anything worth being remembered. My answer to this is: nonsense! *Every* life is worth celebrating, even if it is only by a small number of people. I once met with family members in the home of a woman who had died and did not want a service because she didn't think she had done anything worth remembering and didn't want to inconvenience anyone by having them come to a service. Almost her entire family came, and we spent over an hour and a half telling stories of her life and how significant she had been to them. Some of the most meaningful services I have ever attended had just a handful of people in attendance.

Some people want to avoid a funeral or memorial because they were never "religious" and don't want to look hypocritical. I would argue that it is never too late to make one's peace with God and even the person with a so called "deathbed conversion" deserves to be remembered in an appropriate way.

Some people want to spare their loved ones the expense and emotional toll of having a funeral or memorial. This is a generous thought, but I have never met family members who regretted the time and money spent on a memorial for someone they loved. I have met several though, who wished they had done more when their loved one died.

What Is the Difference between a Funeral and a Memorial Service?

A funeral is usually held just a few days (usually no more than three in North America) after the death. Jewish and Muslim funerals are usually held within twenty-four hours of the death. At a funeral, the body or cremated remains of the deceased is present. Sometimes the lid of the casket is open and sometimes it is closed, depending on the wishes of the

family, their religion's teaching, and the condition of the body — especially if the death is due to an accident. Funerals can be held in churches,
synagogues, temples, mosques, funeral homes, or some other meaningful,
dignified place. Some states still allow burial on private property and a
funeral at the gravesite is be another possibility. A funeral is usually led
or "performed" by a minister, rabbi, imam, pastor, priest, or other religious
figure, though they are sometimes conducted by friends, family, or fraternal organizations. In the case of a prominent person, people who were
professional friends or important individuals in that person's field of work
or service may be asked to speak.

A memorial service is much like a funeral except that it takes place
several days (sometimes weeks) after the death. Also, the body or cremated
remains are not present at a memorial service.

The reasons for having a memorial service rather than a funeral are
many, but usually have to do with the convenience of those who will be
attending. Memorials are usually scheduled to make it easier for people
who live out of town to attend. I once held a memorial service in Cleveland
for a prominent individual who had made his fortune in Oklahoma City,
where he died, had his funeral and was buried. But before he moved
west, he had made many friends and had many family members in Ohio
where he had been born. Each service was well attended, and a video
documentary of his life shown at the memorial service helped the people
in Ohio feel that they had been present at the celebration of his life in
Oklahoma.

Another reason for a memorial is that the body sometimes cannot be
present. This happens when a body is lost, say at sea, or is destroyed by a
fire, airplane crash, or explosion as in the 9/11 disasters.

More often that not, burial is held before a memorial service, sometimes
with just family and close friends in attendance, though sometimes burial
follows a memorial. Though practices may vary from community to community, my experience has been that the burial follows immediately after
the funeral is over. Sometimes, say in the case of a very small family or an
elderly person who has little family and few friends still alive, the funeral
and burial are combined in what is called a "graveside service" held at the

cemetery. The prayers normally said at the graveside can be incorporated into the service at the funeral home or house of worship, in which case no service would be held at the cemetery at all. Sometimes, there is a reason to delay burial. I remember one funeral when the burial had to wait for several months because the cemetery was being moved to make way for highway construction. Sometimes, especially in the northern states, the ground is frozen and so burials have to wait till the spring. In any case, if there is a reason to delay a burial, the funeral home will provide for secure and dignified storage of the body and casket.

People sometimes ask if they can have a funeral and still donate their organs or whole body to science or for transplantation. The answer is yes. Let the funeral home know of your wishes and it will make arrangements. In the case of organ transplantation, the organs can be "harvested" in such a way as to be unnoticeable even if you want to have a viewing or open-casket funeral. In the case of whole body donation, arrangements can often be made to hold the body for a short while to allow for a funeral before it is sent on to the institution to which it was donated. Medical school and research facilities that use human bodies for teaching almost always hold a funeral or memorial for the bodies after they are done with them. Often family members are invited to attend these services. Ask your funeral director or the facility to which you wish to make a donation what their policy is.

Another option for families is to have a body available for viewing and a traditional funeral, and then have the body cremated. Again, speak to your funeral home for details.

It is my impression, and that of funeral directors I have talked to, that more and more families are opting for cremation. One reason for this is cost. Another reason is that our attitudes toward death have changed. Once graveyards were places one went to feel comforted by being in the presence of their loved ones' remains, but that is less the case these days. Today people are as likely to ask to have their ashes sprinkled in the mountains, the ocean, their favorite city, or some other place that holds meaning as they are to ask to have them buried in a traditional family plot.

What Should Happen at a Funeral or Memorial Service?

As far as the "look" of the service, funerals and memorials are about the same except for the presence of the body. In either case, three elements should be included to make the service meaningful to those who attend. First, celebrate and give thanks for the life of the person who has died. Someone once told me that we don't have funerals because someone died; we have them because someone lived. This celebration can take several forms. In a religious service, there are usually prayers that include words of thanksgiving for the life of the person who has died. In both religious and more secular services there is usually a eulogy. Eulogy comes from a Greek word meaning to praise; it literally translates as "the good word." Eulogies can be given by almost anyone, but usually are offered by clergypersons, close friends or business associates, and sometimes by close family members. Usually there are only one or two eulogies offered, though, in the case of a prominent person, several may be included. More and more I see the use of photographs and video to capture and remember a person's life. One woman's family brought in a display of her handicrafts as a way to share this important aspect of her life. These displays are sometimes included in the ceremony, but are usually present on display at a gathering of family and friends before or after the service.

The second element that should be present at a funeral or memorial is the acknowledgment of death. Yes, you are gathered because someone has lived, but you are also gathered because someone has died. The mystery and awe of death should be acknowledged through prayer, hymns, music, or some other means. The reality of our loss needs to be openly and publicly recognized so that we can incorporate the loss into our lives and grow from it.

The final element that needs to be included at a funeral or memorial is the chance to acknowledge and express our grief. Again this can take various forms. Scriptures, poems, or other writings that express the depth of our loss can be read. Often music or songs can express a grief that is unable to be expressed by mere words. Along with the expression of our grief, there should be some indication that healing does go on. Wholeness returns after the brokenness of loss. In religious funerals this often takes the form of prayers of hope or hymns proclaiming the promise of an afterlife with God. People should leave your service with a sense of hope.

Music is often a major part of a funeral or memorial. Appropriate music usually precedes and often follows a funeral or memorial service. Often one of more songs are played or sung during the service as well. I have made several suggestions in appendixes B and C of hymns and songs that might be used.

People sometimes wonder how long a funeral or memorial should last. It is really up to you. I've held some graveside services in the snow and rain that were only ten or fifteen minutes long. The funeral in Detroit when Rosa Parks died lasted over eight hours. Generally, a funeral or memorial is thirty to forty-five minutes long. Some Roman Catholic services are longer if the Eucharist (Holy Communion) is included. I generally advise people that the service should be long enough to say everything that needs to be said, but not so long that it begins to drag on or become hard for children or the elderly to sit through.

It is often appropriate and usually appreciated for friends and loved ones to gather together after the funeral or memorial to share a meal and have a time to talk. Many churches offer the use of their social halls to members for this purpose. Church social halls may also be made available to non-members. In years past, the women of the church would often offer to prepare and serve the meal. You see this less often now because working women have less time during the day to volunteer to do this. Check with your congregation to see what is possible. Some funeral homes are being built with reception halls where such meals can be served. Your funeral director can help you make arrangements there or may know of some other local hall that is available. Sometimes families like to gather at a favorite restaurant or even at someone's home.

A Thought on Funeral or Memorial Decorum

We live in a "do your own thing" world. Funerals and memorial services should reflect the life of the person being remembered, but thought should also be given to who will be attending. Funeral directors have told me horror stories of funerals with piercingly loud rock music that completely overwhelmed elderly persons in attendance. I once conducted a service for a jazz drummer whose musician friends came and played what can best be described as "cocktail gospel" before the funeral. It was a beautiful gift, but it felt more like a "happy hour" than a funeral. Some people want to be buried with their fishing poles or wearing their favorite team's jersey. Some want their club or fraternal organization to have a major role in their ceremony.

This is all well and good. I ask you though, to try to keep your individualizing on the side of good taste. He might have been your drinking buddy, but the flashing neon "This Bud's for you" sign might be upsetting to the person who knew him as her grandson. You might have all hung out together wearing your jeans, short skirts, and motorcycle colors, but a room full of bikers in full regalia might be a bit intimidating to her uncles and aunts who remember her singing in the church choir as a little girl.

All I'm pleading for is a little sensitivity. One can overdo it with tradition, but one can also overdo it trying to avoid tradition. Tone it down just a little out of deference to those who may come to show their respect and love, but may know him or her in a different way than you do. You can always get together with "the gang" later for a private sendoff in whatever form you like.

Appendix B

Christian Resources
for Funerals and Memorials

Scripture Readings

The following passages from the Bible are appropriate for funeral and memorial services. There are other passages that can be used, but these are a good place to start.

Old Testament

Job 19:23–27	I know that my redeemer lives
Ecclesiastes 3:1–15	To everything there is a time
Psalm 8	What is man that you consider him?
Psalm 15	Who shall dwell in your holy tabernacle?
Psalm 16:5–11	The Lord is my chosen portion
Psalm 23	The Lord is my shepherd, I shall not want
Psalm 27:1, 4–9, 13–14	The Lord is my light and my salvation
Psalm 36	Be a rock of refuge . . . you have seen my affliction
Psalm 39:4–5, 12	Lord, let me know my end
Psalm 42:1–6	As a deer longs for flowing streams
Psalm 43	Give judgment for me, O God
Psalm 46:1–5, 10–11	A very present help in trouble
Psalm 90: 1–10, 12	You have been our dwelling place in all generations

Psalm 91	The one who lives in the shelter of the Most High
Psalm 10	Bless the Lord, O my soul
Psalm 106:1–5	O give thanks to the Lord
Psalm 118	Open the gate of righteousness
Psalm 121	I lift my eyes to the hills from whence comes my help
Psalm 130	Out of the depths I cry to the Lord
Psalm 139:1–12	Whither shall I go from your spirit?
Psalm 145	I will exalt you, O God my King
Psalm 146	Hallelujah! Praise the Lord, O my soul
Isaiah 25:6–9	God will swallow up death forever
Isaiah 26:1–4, 19	God will keep in perfect peace
Isaiah 40:1–11, 28–31	Comfort, comfort, ye my people
Isaiah 40:28–31	They shall mount up like eagles
Isaiah 43:1–3a, 18–19, 25	When you pass through the waters
Isaiah 44:6–8	I am the first and the last
Isaiah 55:1–3, 6–13	The spirit of the Lord is upon me
Isaiah 66:17–25	I create a new heavens and a new earth
Lamentations 3:19–26, 31–36	The Lord is good to those who wait
Daniel 12:1–3	Many of those who sleep in the dust shall awake
Joel 2:12–13, 23–24, 26–29	Turn to me with all your heart

New Testament

Matthew 5:1–12	The beatitudes
Matthew 11:25–30	Hidden from the wise; revealed to babes
Matthew 18:1–5, 10	Who is greatest in the kingdom of heaven?
Matthew 18:21–25	How many times to forgive
Matthew 25:1–13	Wise and foolish virgins
Matthew 25:31–46	The last judgment
Mark 10:13–16	Let the children come to me
Luke 7:11–17	Jesus raises the son of the widow of Nain
Luke 18:15–17	We enter the kingdom as children
Luke 23:33, 39–43	Today you will be with me in paradise
John 3:16–21	God so loved the world
John 5:24–29	Whoever hears and believes has eternal life
John 6:46–58	Whosoever believes in me has eternal life

John 10:11–16	I am the good shepherd
John 11:17–27	I am the resurrection and the life
John 11:38–44	Lazarus raised from the death
John 14:1–6; 25–27	Let not your hearts be troubled
John 15:9–17	My commandment…love one another
Romans 2:12–16	The law written on the heart
Romans 5:1–11	Hope does not disappoint
Romans 6:3–9	Baptized into Christ's death; raised to live with him
Romans 8:14–23; 31–39	Nothing can separate us from the love of God
Romans 14:7–9; 10–12	Whether we live or die, we are the Lord's
1 Corinthians 15:3–8; 12–20	Christ raised from death
1 Corinthians 15:20–24	In Christ shall all be made alive
1 Corinthians 15:35–38; 42–44; 50; 53–58	Death is swallowed in victory
1 Corinthians 15:35–55	The natural body; the spiritual body
1 Corinthians 15:50–57	We shall all be changed
2 Corinthians 4:16–5:1	Visible things transitory; invisible things permanent
2 Corinthians 5:1–5	We have a house not made with hands
Ephesians 1:11–2:1, 4–10	Saved by grace through faith
Philippians 3:7–11	Knowing him and the power of his resurrection
Philippians 3:20–21	Our citizenship is in heaven
Colossians 3:1–17	Set your mind on the things above
1 Thessalonians 4:13–18	The comfort of Christ's coming
1 Timothy 2:8–13	If we died with him, we shall also live with him.
Hebrews 2:14–18	Christ was tempted, yet was without sin
Hebrews 11:1–3, 13–16, 12:1–2	Faith; pilgrimage; the cloud of witnesses
1 Peter 1:3–12	Without seeing Christ you loved him
1 Peter 3:18–22; 4:6	Christ's ministry to the spirits in prison
1 John 3:1–3	We are children of God
Revelation 7:2–3; 9–17	They who came out of the tribulation
Revelation 14:1–3; 6–7; 12–13	Rest for the saints
Revelation 21:1–4; 22–25; 22:3–5	A new heaven and a new earth
Revelation 22:1–5	The Lord God will be their light

Hymns and Religious Songs

Some people find that singing is a way to express what is otherwise hard to express. The following are some Christian hymns that you might consider using at a memorial or funeral. Again, the list is not complete, but it will get you started.

A Mighty Fortress is Our God

Abide with Me

All My Heart This Night Rejoices

Amazing Grace, How Sweet the Sound

Because He Lives

Beneath the Cross of Jesus

Blessed Assurance, Jesus is Mine

Blessed Be the Ties the Bind

Borning Cry

Christ Is Made the Sure Foundation

Christ, Whose Glory Fills the Skies

Come, Thou Almighty King

Come, Thou Long-expected Jesus

Come, You Thankful People, Come

Christ Is Made the Sure foundation

Crown Him with Many Crowns

For All the Saints

Give to the Winds Your Fears

God of Our Life

Good Christian Men, Rejoice

Great is Thy Faithfulness

Hark, the Herald Angels Sing

He Lives

He Touched Me

He's Got the Whole World In His Hands

His Eye is On the Sparrow

Holy God, We Praise Your Name

Holy, Holy, Holy, Lord God Almighty

Hosanna, Loud Hosanna

How Firm a Foundation

I Greet Thee, Who My Sure Redeemer Art

I to the Hills Will Lift My Eyes

In that Great Gettin' Up Morning

In the Sweet By and By

It Is Well with My Soul

Jesus Christ Is Risen Today

Jesus Loves Me, This I Know

Joyful, Joyful, We Adore Thee

Just a Closer Walk with Thee

Leaning on the Everlasting Arms

Lift Every Voice and Sing

Near to the Heart of God

O For a Thousand Tongues to Sing

O Love That Wilt Not Let Me Go

Oh Lord, You Are Our God and King

On Eagle's Wings

Onward, Christian Soldiers

Our God, Our Help in Ages Past

Praise We Our Maker

Praise, My Soul the King of Heaven

Precious Lord, Take My Hand

Rock of Ages

Shall We Gather at the River?

Soon and Very Soon

Standing on the Promises

Sweet Hour of Prayer

The Lord Is My Shepherd

The Solid Rock

There Is a Balm in Gilead

We Come unto Our Father God

We Greet You, Sure Redeemer

What a Friend We Have in Jesus

When the Saints Go Marching In

Will the Circle Be Unbroken?

Appendix C

Popular Resources for Funerals and Memorials

Poems and Other Readings

The following poems and songs have been used in both religious and more secular funerals and memorial services. Again, consider this list simply a starting place.

Autumn Rain
(MARY E. FRYE, 1905)

> Do not stand by my grave and weep.
> I am not there, I do not sleep.
> I am a thousand winds that blow,
> I am the diamond glints upon the snow.
> I am the sunlight on ripened grain and
> I am the gentle autumn rain.
> When you awaken in the morning's hush,
> I am that swift uplifting rush,
> Of quiet birds in circled flight.
> I am the soft star that shines at night.
> Do not stand by my grave and cry,
> I am not there, I did not die.

I'm Free

LINDA JO JACKSON

Don't grieve for me, for now I'm free
I'm following the path God has laid you see.
I took His hand when I heard him call
I turned my back and left it all.

I could not stay another day
To laugh, to love, to work, to play.
Tasks left undone must stay that way
I found that peace at the close of day.

If my parting has left a void
Then fill it with remembered joy.
A friendship shared, a laugh, a kiss
Oh yes, these things I too will miss.

Be not burdened with times of sorrow
I wish you the sunshine of tomorrow.
My life's been full, I savored much
Good friends, good times, a loved one's touch.

Perhaps my time seemed all too brief
Don't lengthen it now with undue grief.
Lift up your hearts and peace to thee
God wanted me now; He set me free.

Gone from My Sight

HENRY VAN DYKE (1852–1933)

I am standing upon the seashore.
A ship at my side spreads her white
sails to the morning breeze and starts
for the blue ocean.

She is an object of beauty and strength.
I stand and watch her until at length

she hangs like a speck of white cloud
just where the sea and sky come
to mingle with each other.

Then, someone at my side says,
"There, she is gone!"

"Gone where?"
Gone from my sight. That is all.
She is just as large in mast and hull
and spar as she was when she left my side
and she is just as able to bear her
load of living freight to her destined port.
Her diminished size is in me, not in her.

And just at the moment when someone
at my side says, "There, she is gone!"
There are other eyes watching her coming,
and other voices ready to take up the glad
shout:
"Here she comes!"
And that is dying.

Requiem

Robert Louis Stevenson (1850–94)

Under the wide and starry sky,
Dig the grave and let me lie.
Glad did I live and gladly die,
And I laid me down with a will.

This be the verse you grave for me:
Here he lies where he longed to be;
Home is the sailor, home from the sea,
And the hunter home from the hill.

Remember

CHRISTINA GEORGINA ROSSETTI (1830–94)

Remember me when I am gone away,
Gone far away into the silent land;
When you can no more hold me by the hand,
Nor I half turn to go, yet turning stay.
Remember me when no more, day by day,
You tell me of our future that you planned:
Only remember me; you understand
It will be late to counsel then or pray.
Yet if you should forget me for a while
And afterwards remember, do not grieve:
For if the darkness and corruption leave
A vestige of the thoughts that I once had,
Better by far you should forget and smile
Than that you should remember and be sad.

To Those I Love

ISLA PASCHAL RICHARDSON

If I should ever leave you,
Whom I love
To go along the silent way...
Grieve not.
Nor speak of me with tears.
But laugh and talk of me
As if I were beside you there.

(I'd come...I'd come,
Could I but find a way!
But would not tears
And grief be barriers?)

And when you hear a song
Or see a bird I loved,
Please do not let the thought of me

Be sad ... for I am loving you
Just as I always have ...

You were so good to me!
There are so many things
I wanted still to do ...
So many things I wanted to say
to you ... Remember that
I did not fear. ... It was
Just leaving you
That was so hard to face.

We cannot see beyond. ...
But this I know:
I loved you so ...
'twas heaven here with you

In Memory

JOYCE KILMER (1886–1918)

Serene and beautiful and very wise,
Most erudite in curious Grecian lore,
You lay and read your learned books, and bore
A weight of unshed tears and silent sighs.
The song within your heart could never rise
Until love bade it spread its wings and soar.
Nor could you look on Beauty's face before
A poet's burning mouth had touched your eyes.

Love is made out of ecstasy and wonder;
Love is a poignant and accustomed pain.
It is a burst of Heaven-shaking thunder;
It is a linnet's fluting after rain.
Love's voice is through your song;
above and under
And in each note to echo and remain

A red rose is His Sacred Heart,
a white rose is His face,
And His breath has turned the barren
world to a rich and flowery place.
He is the Rose of Sharon,
His gardener am I,
And I shall drink His fragrance
in Heaven when I die.

To My Dear and Loving Husband
ANNE BRADSTREET (1612–72)

If ever two were one, then surely we.
If ever man were loved by wife, then thee;
If ever wife was happy in a man,
Compare with me, ye women, if you can.
I prize thy love more than whole mines of gold,
Or all the riches that the East doth hold.
My love is such that rivers cannot quench,
Nor aught by love from thee give recompense.
Thy love is such I can no way repay;
The heavens reward thee manifold, I pray.
Then while we live, in love let's so persever,
That when we live no more we may live ever.

Turn Again to Life
MARY LEE HALL

If I should die and leave you here a while,
be not like others sore undone,
who keep long vigil by the silent dust.
For my sake turn again to life and smile,
nerving thy heart and trembling hand
to do something to comfort other hearts than thine.
Complete these dear unfinished tasks of mine
and I perchance may therein comfort you.

Prayer of St. Francis

FRANCIS OF ASSISI (1182–1226)

Lord, make me an instrument of your peace;
Where there is hatred, let me sow love;
Where there is injury, pardon;
Where there is doubt, faith;
Where there is despair, hope;
Where there is darkness, light;
Where there is sadness, joy.

O Divine Master, grant that I may seek not so much to be consoled,
      as to console;
to be understood as to understand;
to be loved as to love;
for it is in giving that we receive;
it is in pardoning that we are pardoned;
and it is in dying that we are born to Eternal Life. Amen.

Old Irish Toast

ANONYMOUS

May you have food and raiment,
A soft pillow for your head,
May you be forty years in heaven
Before the devil knows you're dead.

The Road Not Taken

ROBERT FROST (1874–1973)

Two roads diverged in a yellow wood,
And sorry I could not travel both
And be one traveler, long I stood
And looked down one as far as I could
To where it bent in the undergrowth;

Then took the other, as just as fair
And having perhaps the better claim,

Because it was grassy and wanted wear;
Though as for that, the passing there
Had worn them really about the same,

And both that morning equally lay
In leaves no step had trodden black,
Oh, I kept the first for another day!
Yet knowing how way leads on to way,
I doubted if I should ever come back.

I shall be telling this with a sigh
Somewhere ages and ages hence:
Two roads diverged in a wood, and I
I took the one less traveled by,
And that has made all the difference.

Not In Vain
EMILY DICKINSON (1837–86)

If I can stop one heart from breaking,
I shall not live in vain:
If I can ease one life the aching,
Or cool one pain,
Or help one fainting robin
Unto his nest again,
I shall not live in vain.

Crossing the Bar
ALFRED, LORD TENNYSON (1809–92)

Sunset and evening star,
And one clear call for me!
And may there be no moaning of the bar,
When I put out to sea,

But such a tide as moving seems asleep,
Too full for sound and foam,

When that which drew from out the boundless deep
Turns again home.

Twilight and evening bell
And after that the dark!
And may there be no sadness of farewell,
When I embark;

For though from out our bourne of Time and Place
The flood may bear me far,
I hope to see my Pilot face to face
When I have crossed the bar.

If

RUDYARD KIPLING (1856–1936)

If you can keep your head when all about you
Are losing theirs and blaming it on you;
If you can trust yourself when all men doubt you,
But make allowance for their doubting too:
If you can wait and not be tired by waiting,
Or, being lied about, don't deal in lies,
Or being hated don't give way to hating,
And yet don't look too good, nor talk too wise;

If you can dream — and not make dreams your master;
If you can think — and not make thoughts your aim,
If you can meet with Triumph and Disaster
And treat those two impostors just the same;
If you can bear to hear the truth you've spoken
Twisted by knaves to make a trap for fools,
Or watch the things you gave your life to, broken,
And stoop and build 'em up with worn-out tools;

If you can make one heap of all your winnings
And risk it on one turn of pitch-and-toss,
And lose, and start again at your beginnings,

And never breathe a word about your loss:
If you can force your heart and nerve and sinew
To serve your turn long after they are gone,
And so hold on when there is nothing in you
Except the Will which says to them: "Hold on!"

If you can talk with crowds and keep your virtue,
Or walk with Kings — nor lose the common touch,
If neither foes nor loving friends can hurt you,
If all men count with you, but none too much:
If you can fill the unforgiving minute
With sixty seconds' worth of distance run,
Yours is the Earth and everything that's in it,
And, which is more — you'll be a Man, my son!

Funeral Poems for Babies or Children

Songs of the Death of Children (Kindertotenlieder)
FRIEDRICH RUCKERT (1788–1866)

You must not shut the night inside you,
But endlessly in light the dark immerse.
A tiny lamp has gone out in my tent —
I bless the flame that warms the universe.

Epitaph on a Child
THOMAS GRAY (1716–71)

Here, freed from pain, secure from misery, lies
A child, the darling of his parents' eyes:
A gentler Lamb ne'er sported on the plain,
A fairer flower will never bloom again:
Few were the days allotted to his breath;
Now let him sleep in peace his night of death.

Little Angels (1)
AUTHOR UNKNOWN

When God calls little children to dwell with Him above,
We mortals sometime question the wisdom of His love.
For no heartache compares with the death of one small child
Who does so much to make our world, seem wonderful and mild
Perhaps God tires of calling the aged to his fold,
So He picks a rosebud, before it can grow old.
God knows how much we need them, and so He takes but few
To make the land of Heaven more beautiful to view.
Believing this is difficult still somehow we must try,
The saddest word mankind knows will always be "Goodbye."
So when a little child departs, we who are left behind
Must realize God loves children, Angels are hard to find.

Little Angels (2)
AUTHOR UNKNOWN

[*Change the name, age, and gender for your own situation*]
God sent an angel to the earth . . .
The sweetest angel too
and for such a tiny little thing,
she had so much to do.
She knew she did not have
much time upon this earth to stay,
so she did not waste a second;
she got started right away.

Her eyes were bright and sparkly,
she took in every turn.
She did not miss a single thing,
because _____ came to learn!
God sent her here to touch the hearts
of those he could not reach . . .
She taught them courage, strength, and faith,

because _____ came to teach.

Her tiny little body
was so full of God above,
you felt it when you held her,
because _____ came to love.

In ____ short months she managed
what many never will.
When she went home to Jesus,
her purpose was fulfilled.
She learned and taught, loved and played,
she learned her lessons well.
I know he was so proud of her
when she went home to dwell.

But when I miss her OH-SO-MUCH,
I can almost hear him say,
please understand, her work was done...
_____ did not come to stay.

Popular Songs

These popular songs may be appropriate for a funeral or memorial service.
I encourage you to be sensitive to the variety of people who will likely be
attending when you decide to use one of these songs.

Song	Artist
A Day without Rain	Enya
A Love Supreme	John Coltrane
All about Our Love	Sade
All You Need is Love	The Beatles
Affirmation	Savage Garden
Amazing Grace	various
Angel	Sarah McLachlan
Angels	Robbie Williams

Beautiful Among Us	Alabama
Beautiful Boy	The Beatles
Beautiful Day	U2
Beautiful In My Eyes	Joshua Kaddison
Because You Loved Me	Celine Dion
Blowing in the Wind	Bob Dylan
Blue Eyes Crying in the Rain	Willie Nelson
Bridge Over Troubled Waters	Simon and Garfunkel
Callin' All Angels	*Pay it Forward* (movie soundtrack)
Candle in the Wind	Elton John
Come Rain or Come Shine	B. B. King
Death is Not the End	Bob Dylan
Don't Look Back in Anger	Oasis
Down to the River to Pray	*O Brother Where Art Thou?* (movie soundtrack)
Dust in the Wind	Kansas
Everybody Hurts	REM
Fanfare for the Common Man	Emerson, Lake, and Palmer
Forever Young	Bob Dylan
Forever Young	Joan Baez
Funeral for a Friend	Elton John
God Bless the Child	Billie Holliday
God Bless the Child	Blood Sweat and Tears
Hero	Mariah Carey
Hey Now, Hey Now	Crowded House
I Don't Want to Miss a Thing	Aerosmith
I Need a Hero	Bonnie Taylor
I Will Always Love You	Whitney Houston
I Will Remember You	Sarah McLachlan
I'll Fly Away	*O Brother Where Art Thou?* movie soundtrack
If Tomorrow Never Comes	Ronan Keating
Jesus is Just Alright with Me	The Doobie Brothers

Knockin' on Heaven's Door	Bob Dylan
Lean on Me	Bill Withers
Let it Be	The Beatles
Let There be Light/Spirits Dancing in the Flesh	Santana
Lonely Stranger	Eric Clapton
Long As I Can See the Light	Credence Clearwater Revival
Looking Through Your Eyes	Leann Rimes
Love Me Tender	Elvis Presley
May it Be	Enya
Memories	Barbra Streisand
Millennium (Lord's) Prayer	Cliff Richard
Missing You	Puff Daddy
Music Box	Mariah Carey
My Father's Eyes	Eric Clapton
My Heart Will Go On	Celine Dion (*Titanic* soundtrack)
My Immortal	Evanescence
My Way	Frank Sinatra
Nothing Compares 2 U	Sinead O' Connor
Nothing Else Matters	Metallica
November Rain	Guns N' Roses
Oceans	Pearl Jam
Oh, Very Young	Cat Stephens
One day at a Time	Patty Newton
One Love	Bob Marley
One Sweet Day	Mariah Carey and Boys II Men
Only Time	Enya
People Get Ready	Curtis Mayfield
Prayer	Celine Dion
Presence of the Lord	Blind Faith (with Eric Clapton)
Put Your Lights On	Santana (with Everlast)
Rainy Day Bells	The Globetrotters
Right Here Waiting	Richard Marx
Runnin' On Faith	Eric Clapton

Save a Prayer	Duran Duran
Stairway to Heaven	Led Zeppelin
Sweet Child of Mine	Guns'n'Roses
Tears in Heaven	Eric Clapton
The Day You Went Away	Wendy Matthews
The Long and Winding Road	The Beatles
The Rose	Bette Midler
The Sweetest Gift	Sade
There You'll Be	Faith Hill
Uncloudy Day	Willie Nelson
Unforgettable	Nat King Cole
What a Wonderful World	Louis Armstrong
What's This Life For	Creed
Walk On	U2
Yesterday	The Beatles
You Lift Me Up	Josh Groban

Other books by The Pilgrim Press

Healing
Insights Series
Donna Schaper
978-0-8298-1703-4 / 48 pages / paper / $6.00

This Insights series booklet discusses five study sessions on the healing narratives from the New Testament.

Job
Insights Series
Raymond Whitfield
0-8298-1557-0 / 48 pages / paper / $5.00

In an accessible way, Whitfield invites readers to ponder such questions as: What is God really like? Why should we worship God? Why do the righteous suffer? *Job* is a brief yet complete guide to the Hebrew Scriptures' book of Job.

Becoming Jesus' Prayer
Transforming Your Life Through the Lord's Prayer
Gregory Palmer, Cindy McCalmont, and Brian Milford
0-8298-1707-7 / 96 pages / paper / $10.00

This wonderful resource invites readers to take a new look at the Lord's Prayer — words so familiar to Christians, yet often muttered without thinking. Each chapter features a story, theological reflection, discussion questions, guidelines for weekly prayer at home and coroporate prayer, and hymn suggestions.

My Loved One is Dying – Revised
The Looking Up Series
John E. Biegert
0-8298-1623-2 / 24 pages / paper / $3.00

A brief book to provide comfort and understanding in a time of grief and anguish.

To order these or any other books from The Pilgrim Press call or write to:

The Pilgrim Press
700 Prospect Avenue East
Cleveland, Ohio 44115-1100

Phone orders: 1-800-537-3394 / Fax orders: 216-736-2206

Please include shipping charges of $5.00 for the first book
and $0.75 for each additional book.

Or order from our websites at
www.thepilgrimpress.com
and
www.unitedchurchpress.com

Prices subject to change without notice.